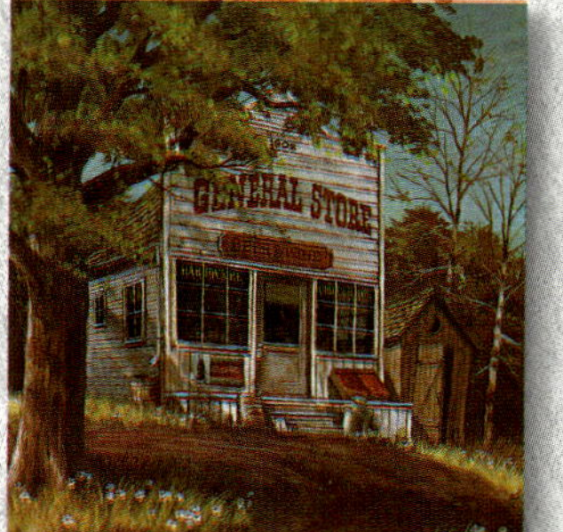

Country Scenes

There is an undeniable charm surrounding a quaint country scene—whether the focus is on a red barn covered in snow, an old-fashioned wagon full of harvest pumpkins, or a quiet farm underneath a blue springtime sky. In this book, you'll learn how to paint a number of country scenes in acrylic, as well as how to create specific moods, seasons, and times of day. You'll also discover easy brush techniques for painting clouds, trees, and skies—and information on creating additional embellishments, such as barrels, windmills, wagons, and fences. Renowned artist Bob Bates demonstrates how to arrange the elements in a scene to create an effective composition, as well as how to change the light source to make a composition more appealing. He also includes tips on taking artistic license and using references for inspiration, making this book an indispensible guide for anyone who wants to capture on canvas the nostalgic charm of country life.

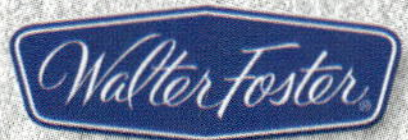

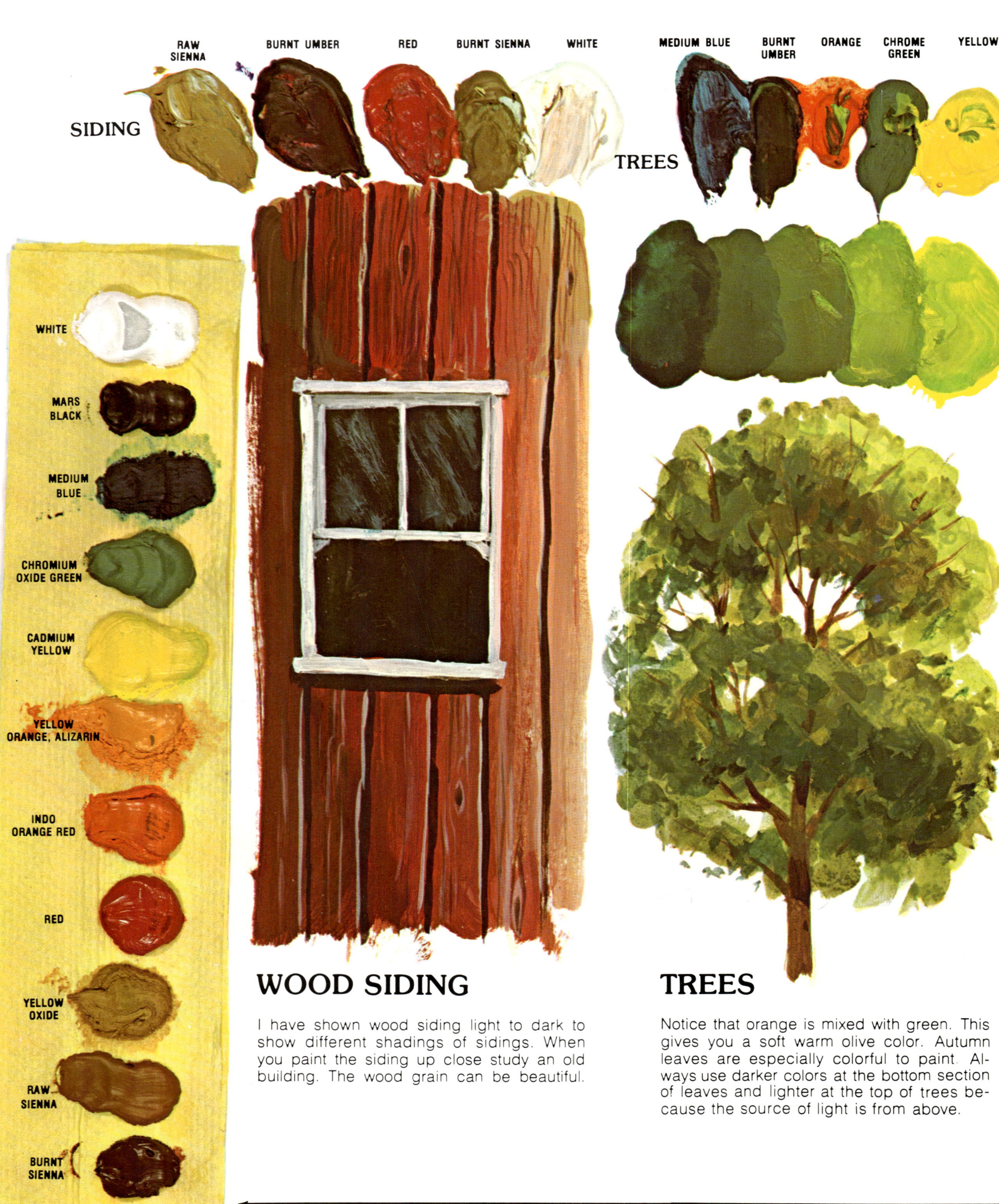

WOOD SIDING

I have shown wood siding light to dark to show different shadings of sidings. When you paint the siding up close study an old building. The wood grain can be beautiful.

TREES

Notice that orange is mixed with green. This gives you a soft warm olive color. Autumn leaves are especially colorful to paint. Always use darker colors at the bottom section of leaves and lighter at the top of trees because the source of light is from above.

PALETTE

Fold a paper towel so you have three thicknesses and then place it on the side of a waxed paper palette. Saturate that towel with water to which you have added a retarding medium. Your paint will stay wet longer this way. Acrylics dry very fast without this retardant. I also use two water jars with retarding medium in them.

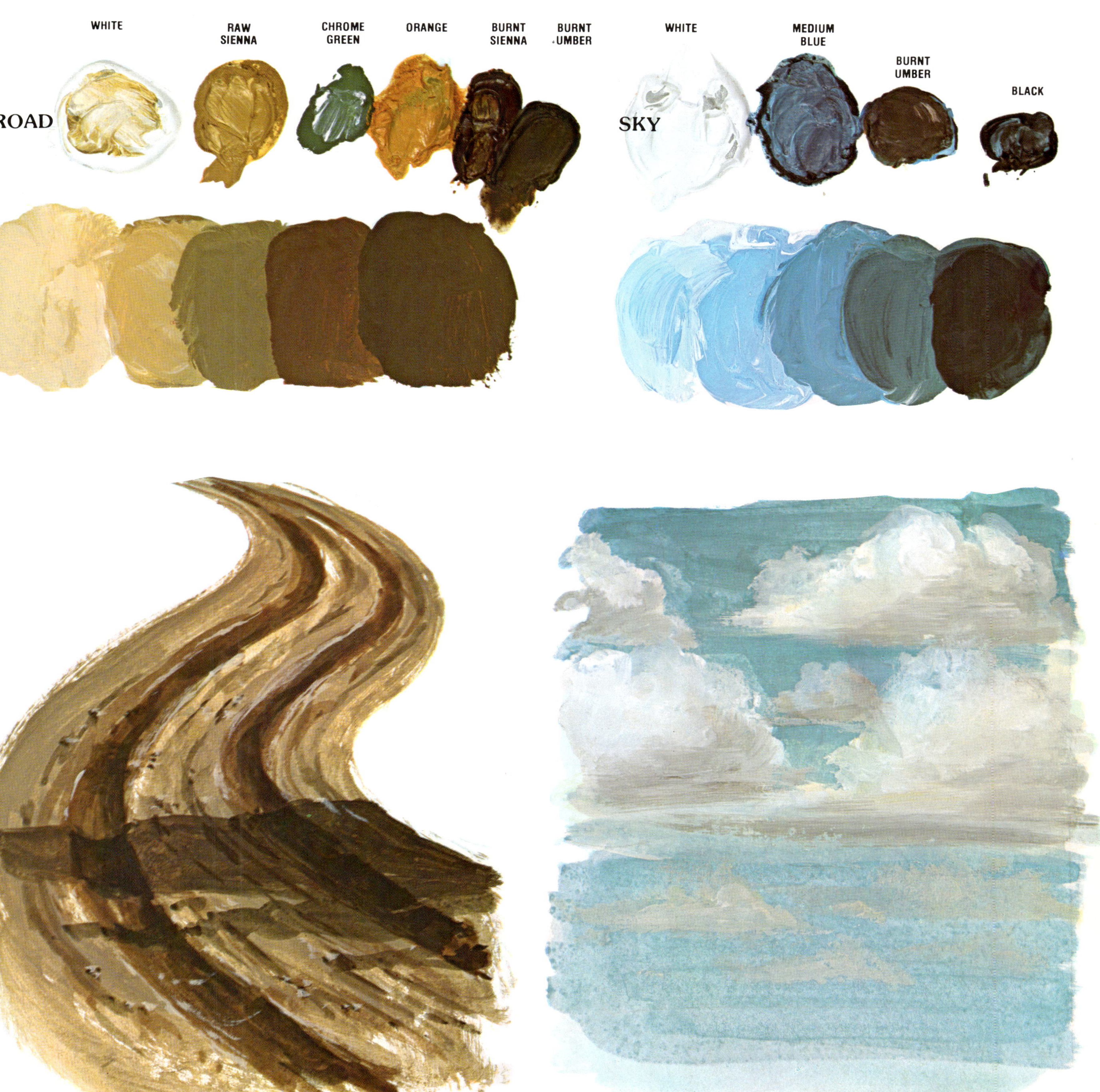

ROADS

A winding road certainly helps a viewer step right into a painting! Keep your vanishing point in mind and you will notice also that if the sun is on your left, the right side of the ruts is always darker and vice-versa. Third dimension is achieved in this way. As shown above, paint a shadow in the same direction, right to left, as it will contribute to the realism of your road.

CLOUDS

Paint your sky first. Medium blue is used in the center, with white toward the bottom. Dark blue is used at the top with a touch of black and dark brown added. When sky is completely dry, add your clouds. The white clouds are flat across the bottom and puffy on top. Leave the shape up to your imagination.

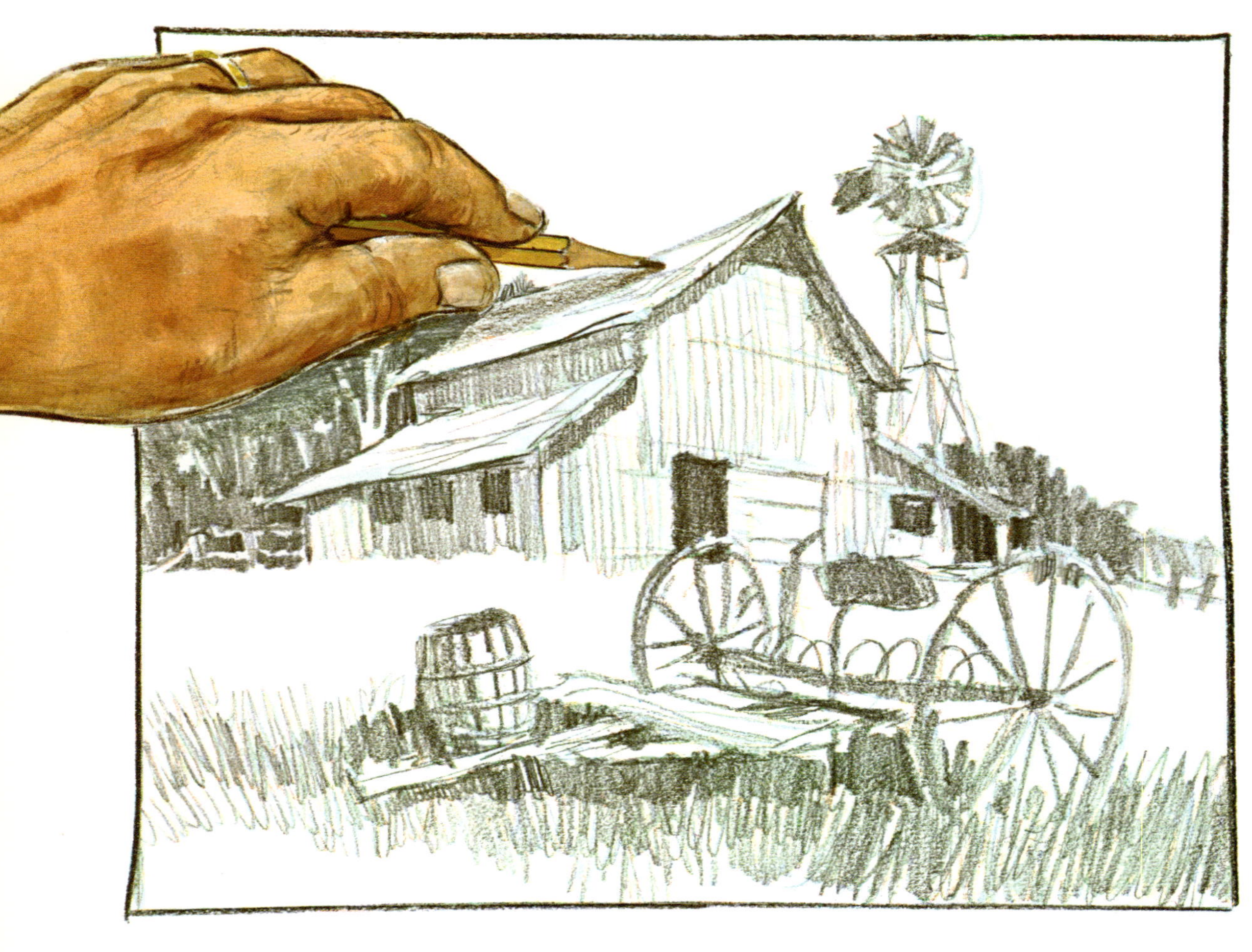

Now we are ready to do a total picture.

On your sketching pad, draw your scene with a pencil using broad strokes. This drawing has dark and light shading, but very little line. Keep in mind the importance of contrast in your picture. Working in pencil helps you see what contrast can do for a painting.

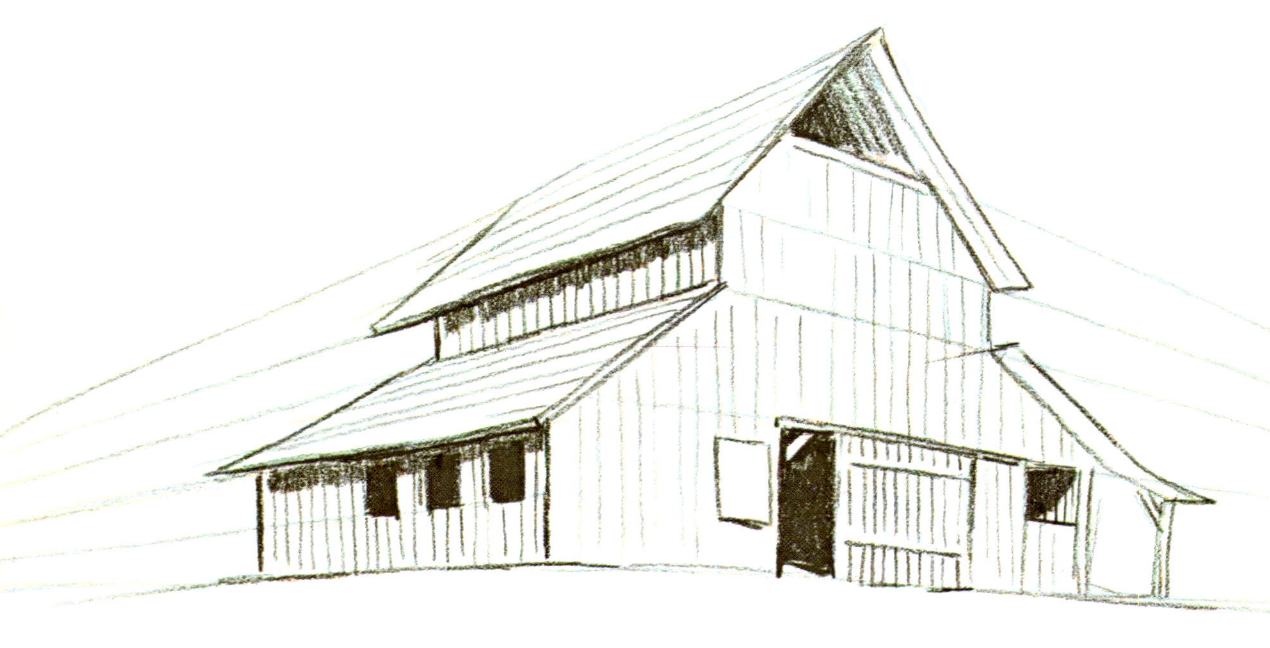

For practice in third dimension on buildings such as this barn, draw very soft lines back to a vanishing point as a guide to the shape of the building. An odd-shaped roof like this can give you trouble if you don't lay it out properly first.

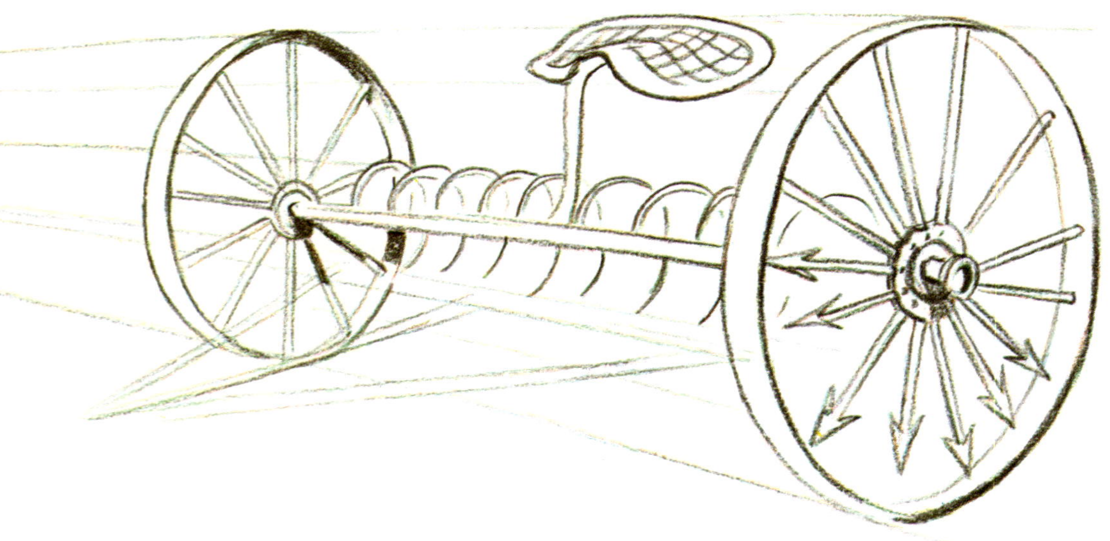

To draw the wheels on this rake, draw an oval not a circle. When you overlap two ovals, it creates the inside and outside of the metal wheel. Be sure your spokes follow in a straight line continuing on the other side of the hub. If you could draw enough lines, every part of this rake would have a vanishing point.

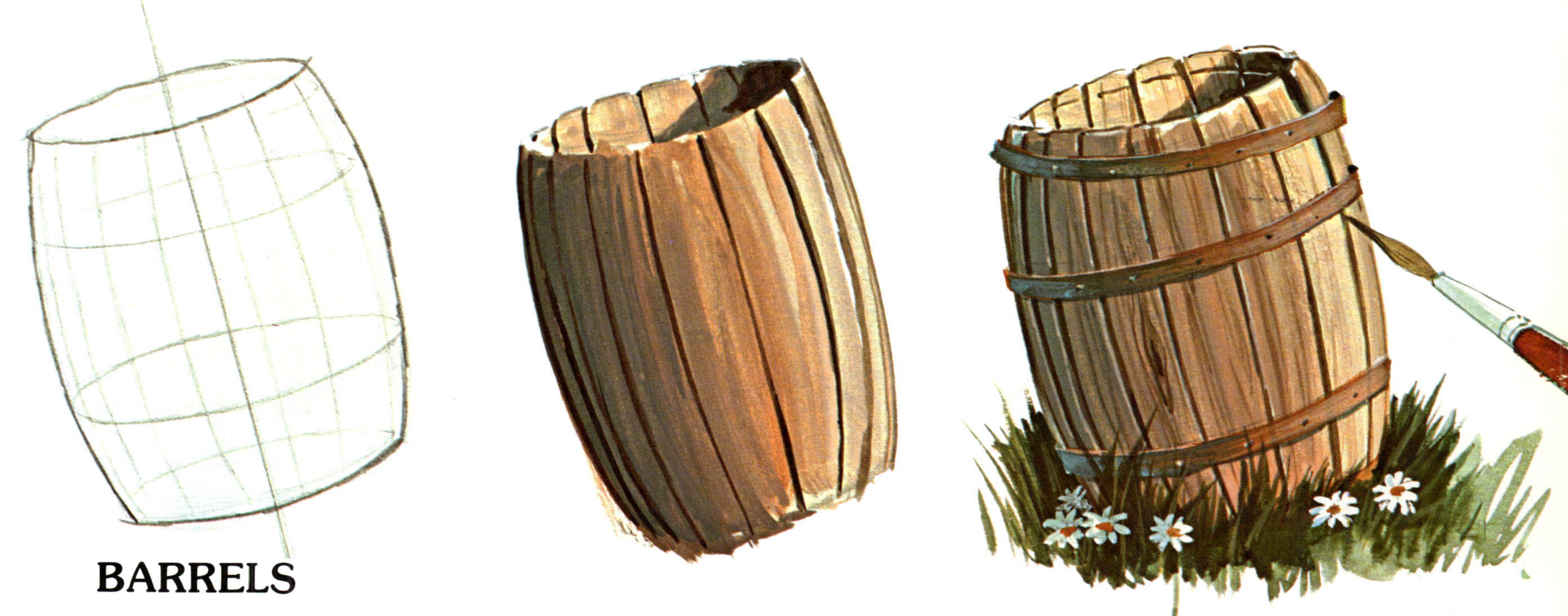

BARRELS

Barrels are fun to draw as long as you think elipses. Your paint strokes must follow that curve. Determine your source of light and add shadow to inside of barrel. The barrel stays are elipses added after the barrel is completely dry.

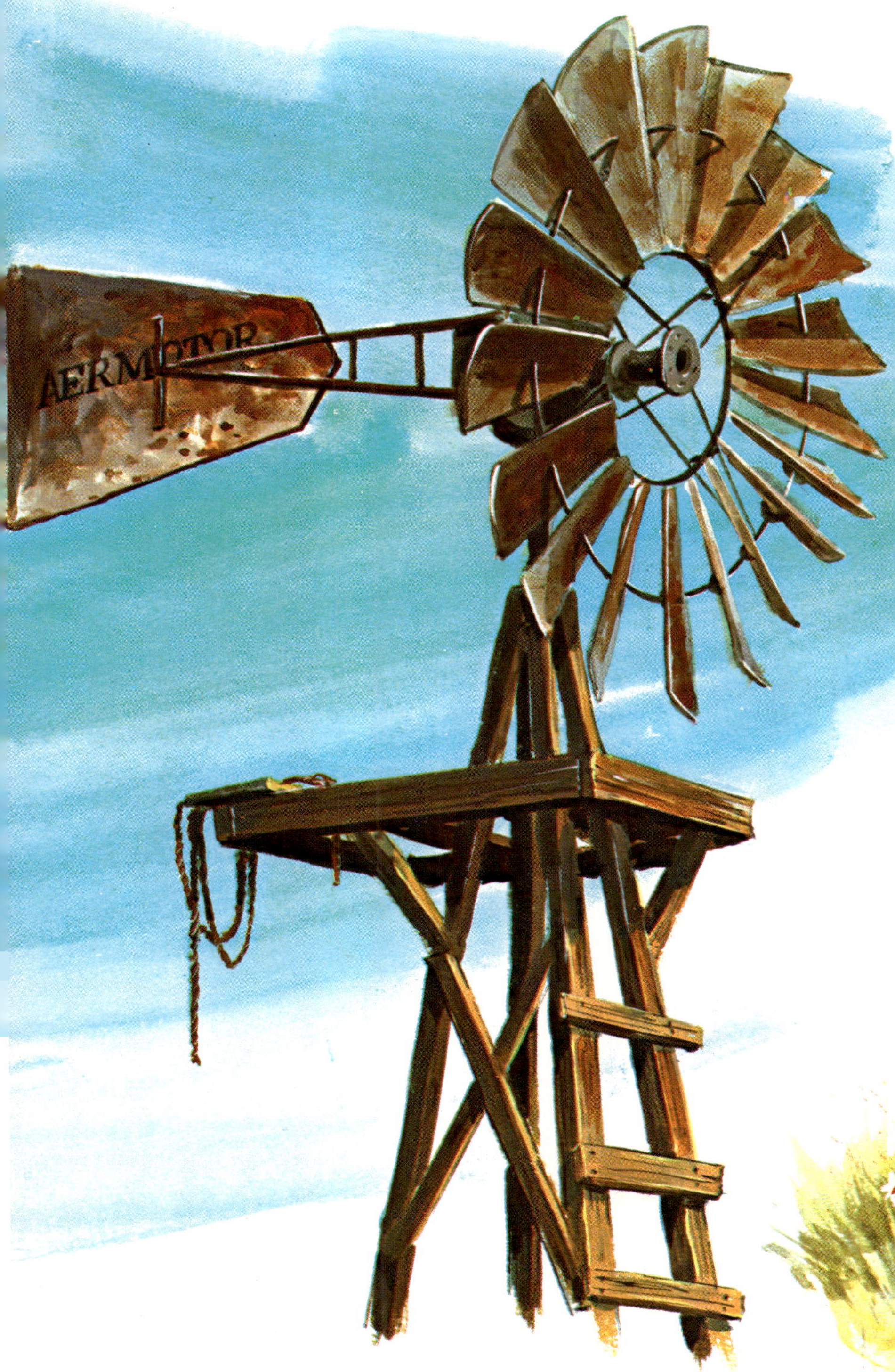

WINDMILLS

If a person studies the shape of the blades of the windmill, he won't have difficulty in reproducing it. Notice how they look different in each position. This is another time when good photos are a must!

EMBELLISHMENTS

Barrels, windmills, and a gate post such as this are great additions to your country scenes adding a certain charm.

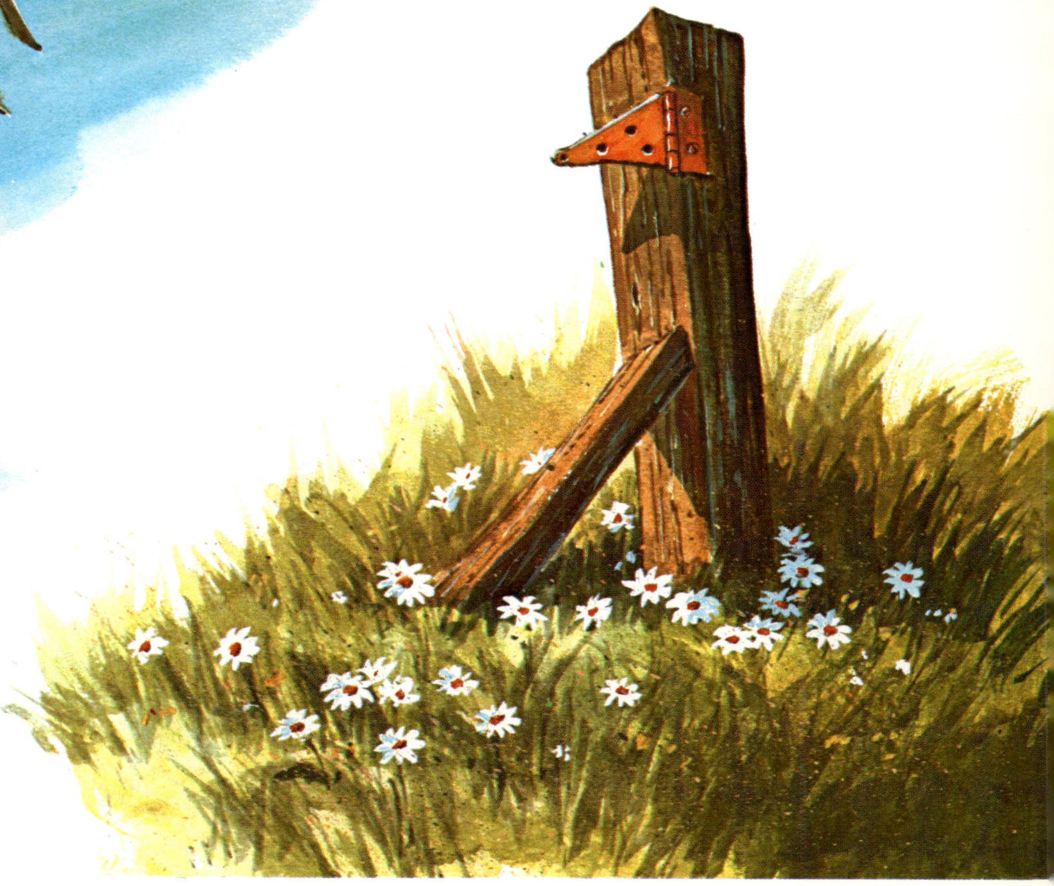

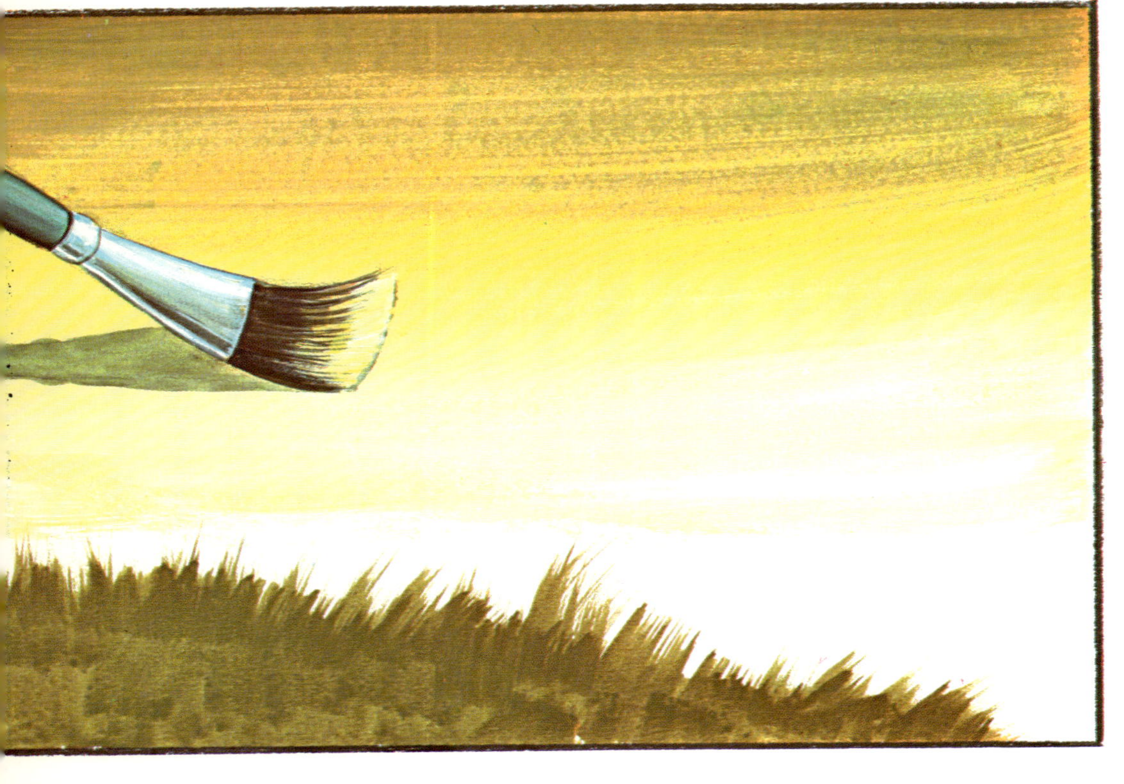

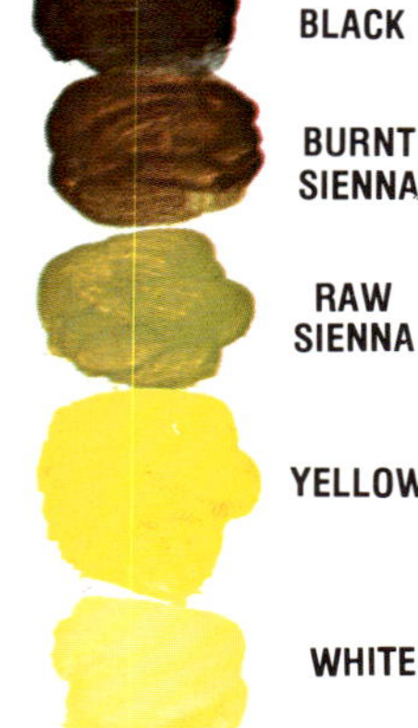

In acrylic I like to paint on untempered masonite. Using an old brush, paint the board with Gesso. When it is half dry rough up the brush strokes with a rag, using a lifting motion. After it dries sand the Gesso with fine sand paper. On the preceding pages you have had practice on barns, windmills, barrels, and a rake. Now let's put them all together.

We'll do the sky first with a flat 1″ brush. Wash the colors from dark at the top to light below.

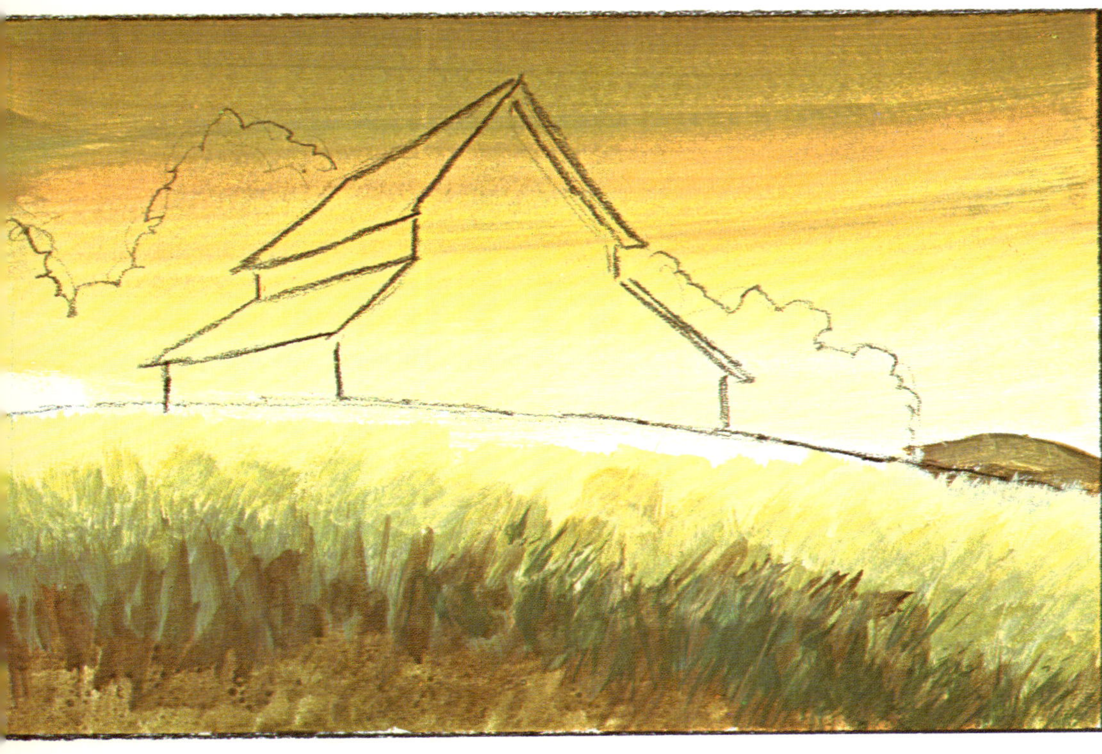

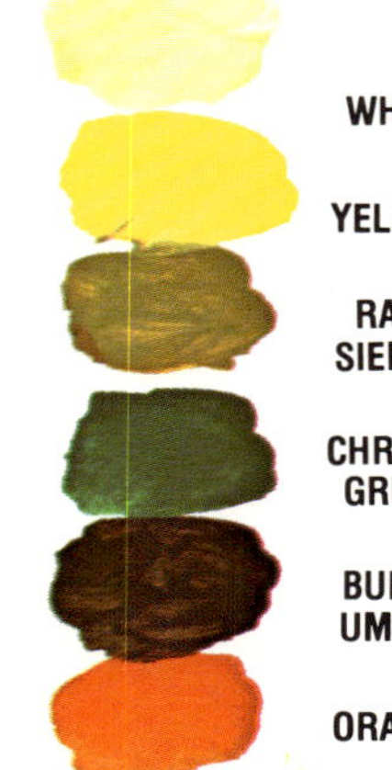

Using the same broad brush, back stroke with a base color as shown. This provides a base for your details which you will add later. At this point, I lightly sketch in my main subject thinking about the vanishing points.

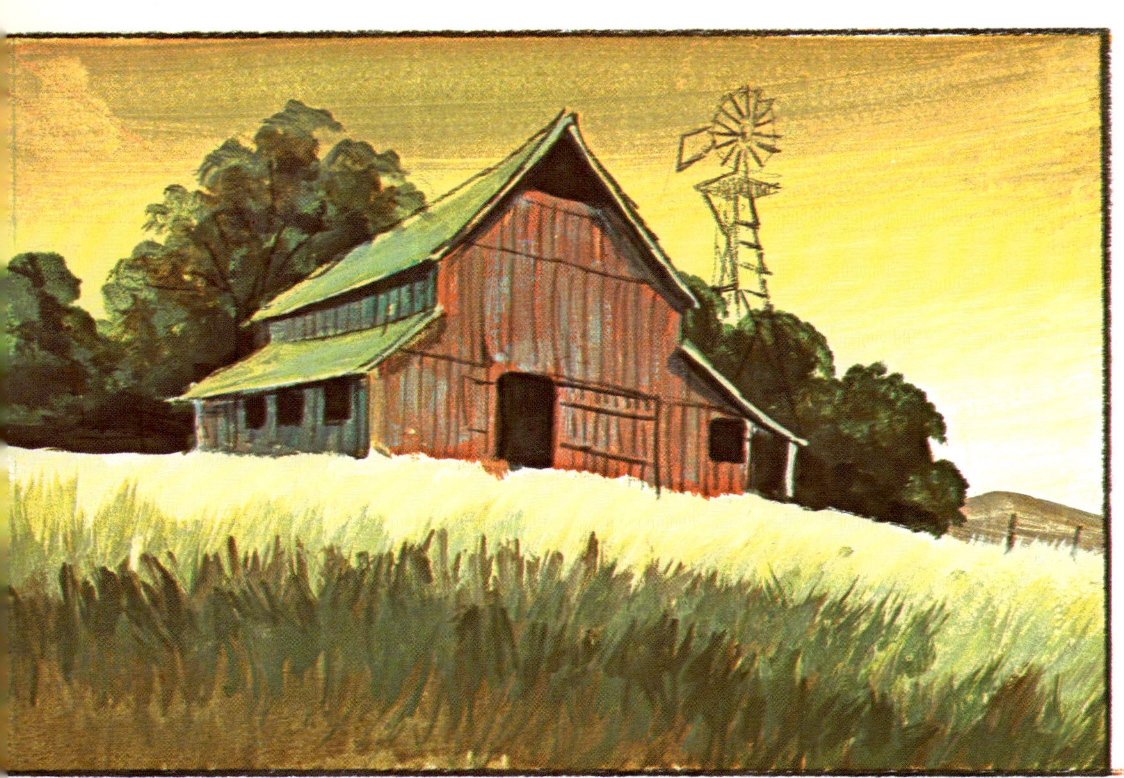

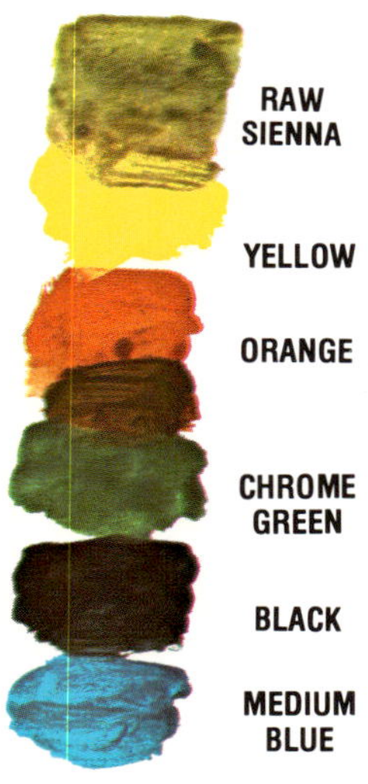

Now you can paint the entire picture with your base colors. You can put in your darks and lights and get a general idea of what it will look like. You can still make changes at this point before your details are added.

Put in any object you think would look good around a farm, keeping in mind your source of light and cast a shadow from each object.

EXTRA TOUCHES

For your details, shadows, etc., remember your practice work on the preceding pages. You might also want to try a little tooth brush splattering. This is done after the painting is completely dry. Use colors like Indo Orange, Yellow Oxide, or Chrome Oxide Green. Dip a tooth brush into paint, draw a pencil or stick across the bristles to splatter it on. Practice on paper first! If your paint gets into the sky or an undesired area, wipe it off immediately.

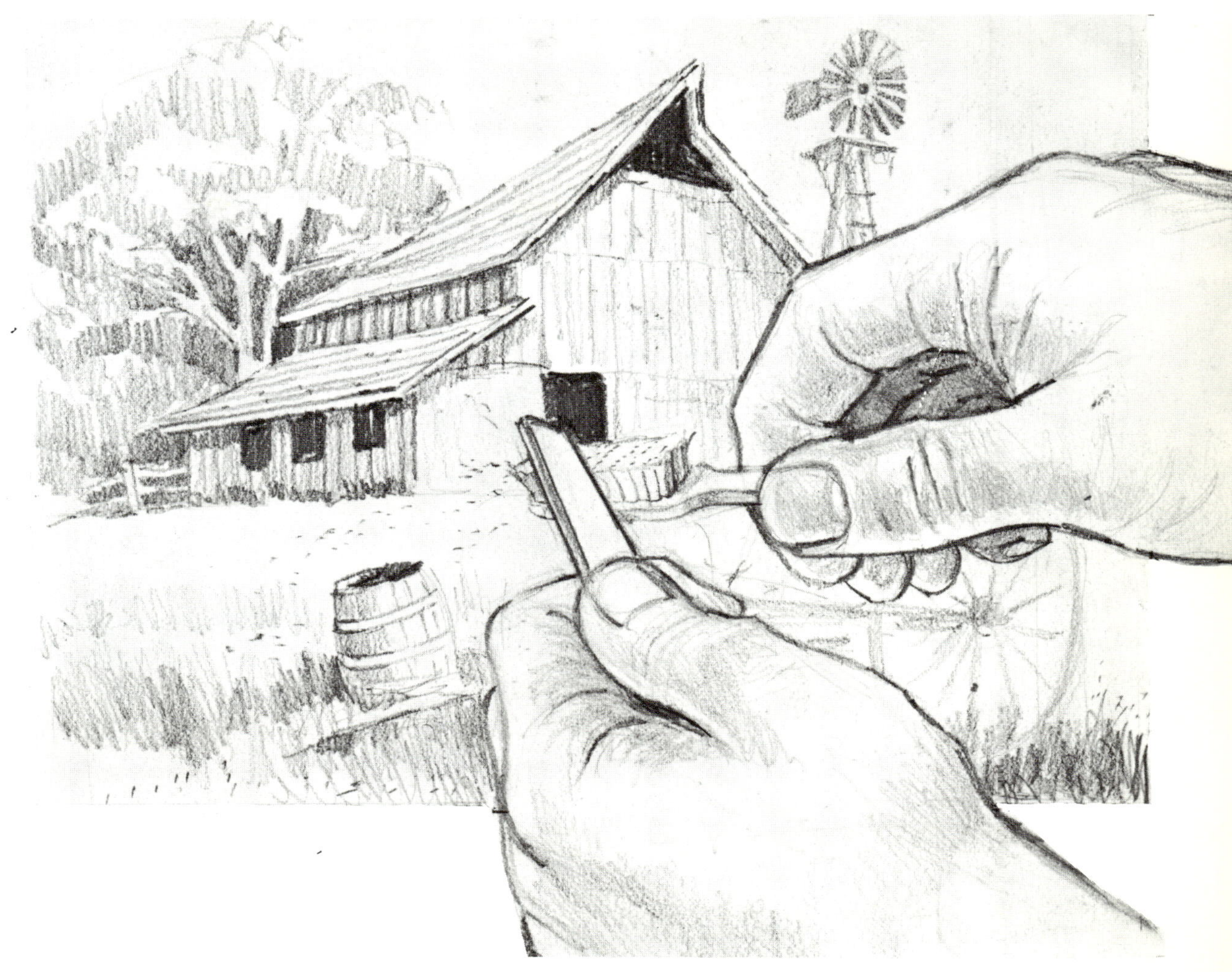

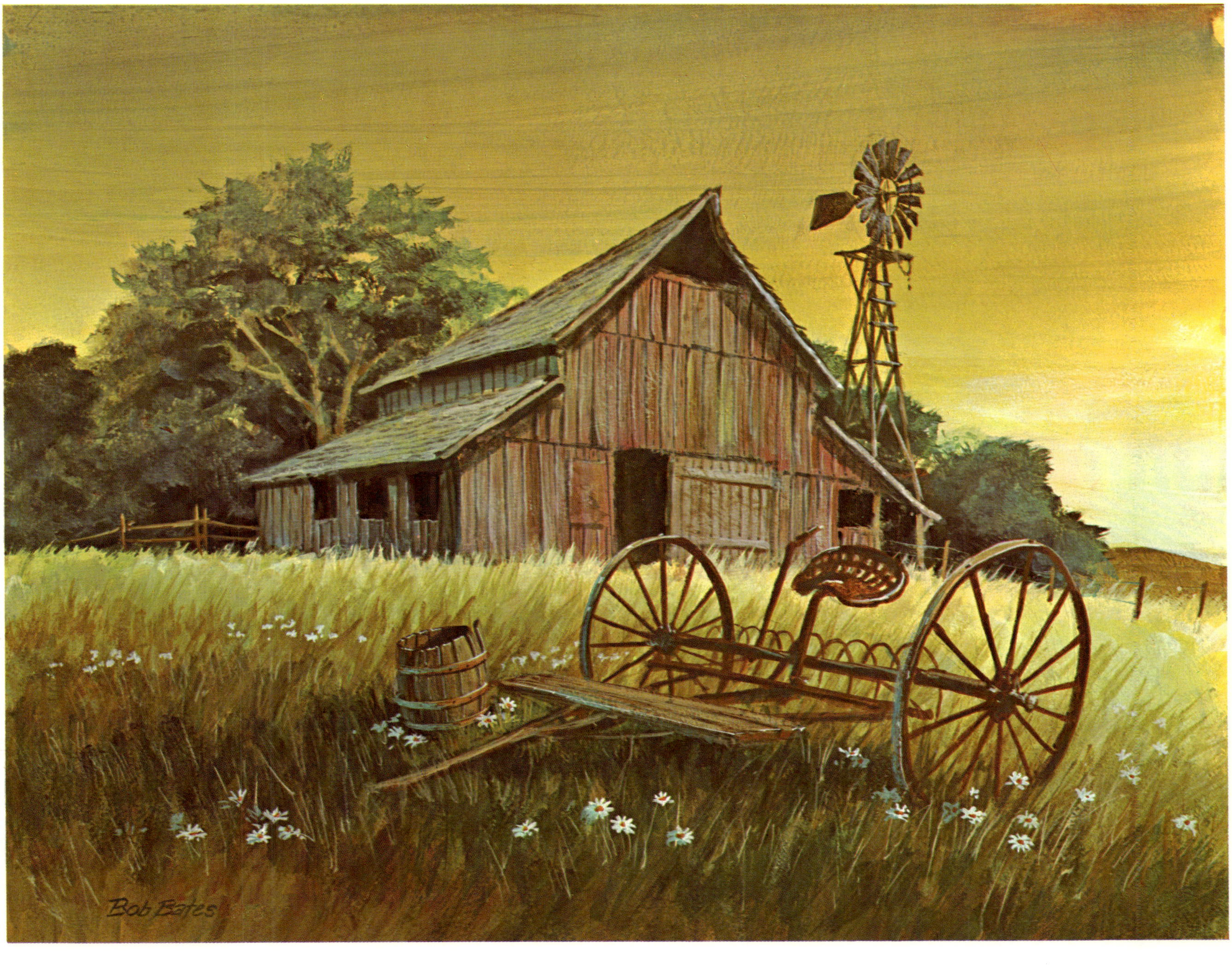

To create a stormy look use Cerulean Blue, Raw Sienna and White with some Black and Medium Blue.

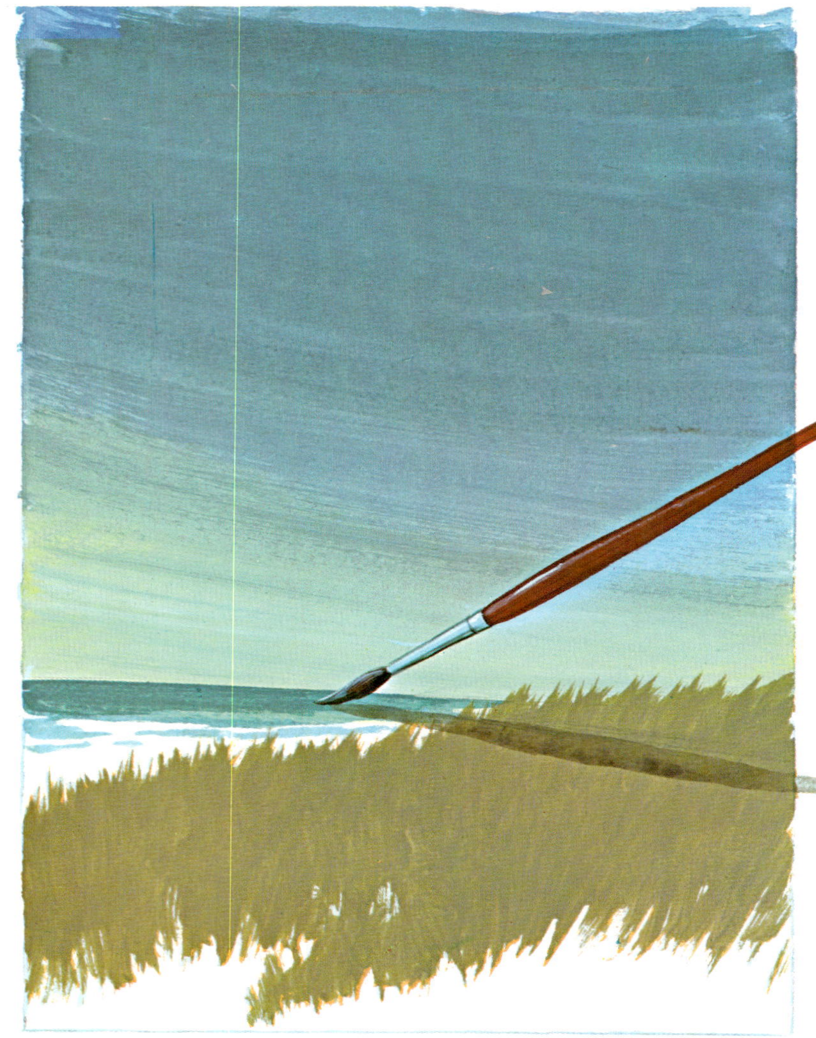

Block in the rest of your painting and leave a space for your lighthouse windows.

THE OLD LIGHTHOUSE

Paint the water and shoreline completely now because the weeds will cover part of it later. Use the same colors in the water as in the sky except darken with Chrome Green.

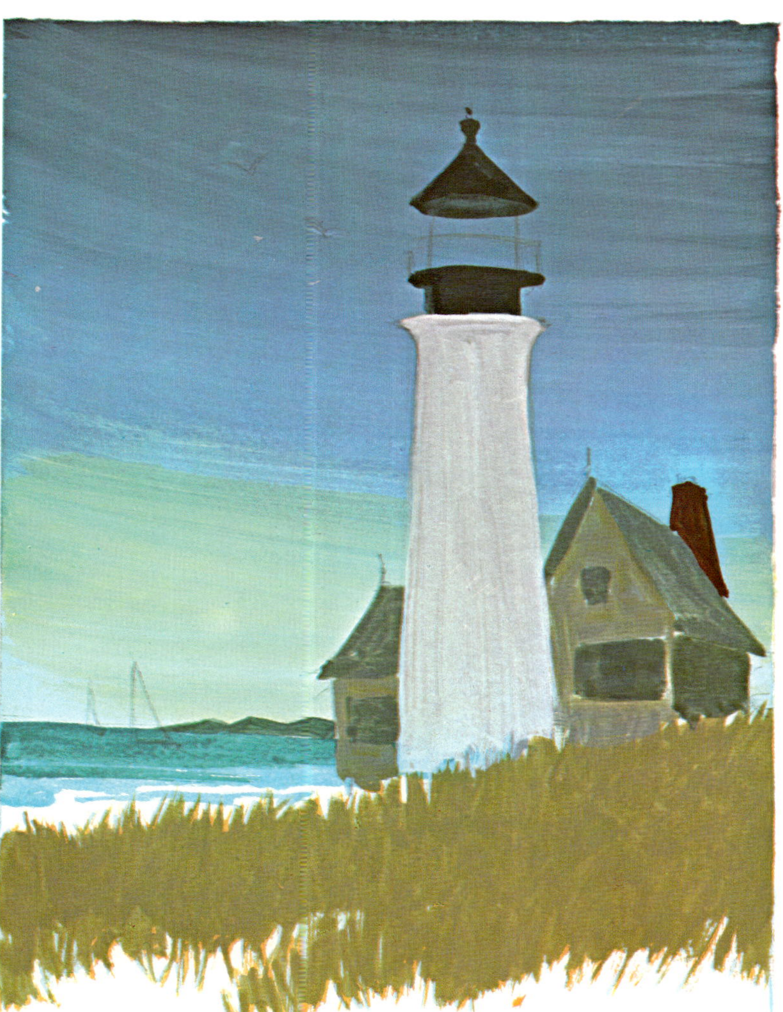

Note the position of the brush to do your backstroke on the weeds. Bend them over to show wind direction. For the window glass, water down your paints to get a thin transparent look to your glass. Your roof and sky should show through.

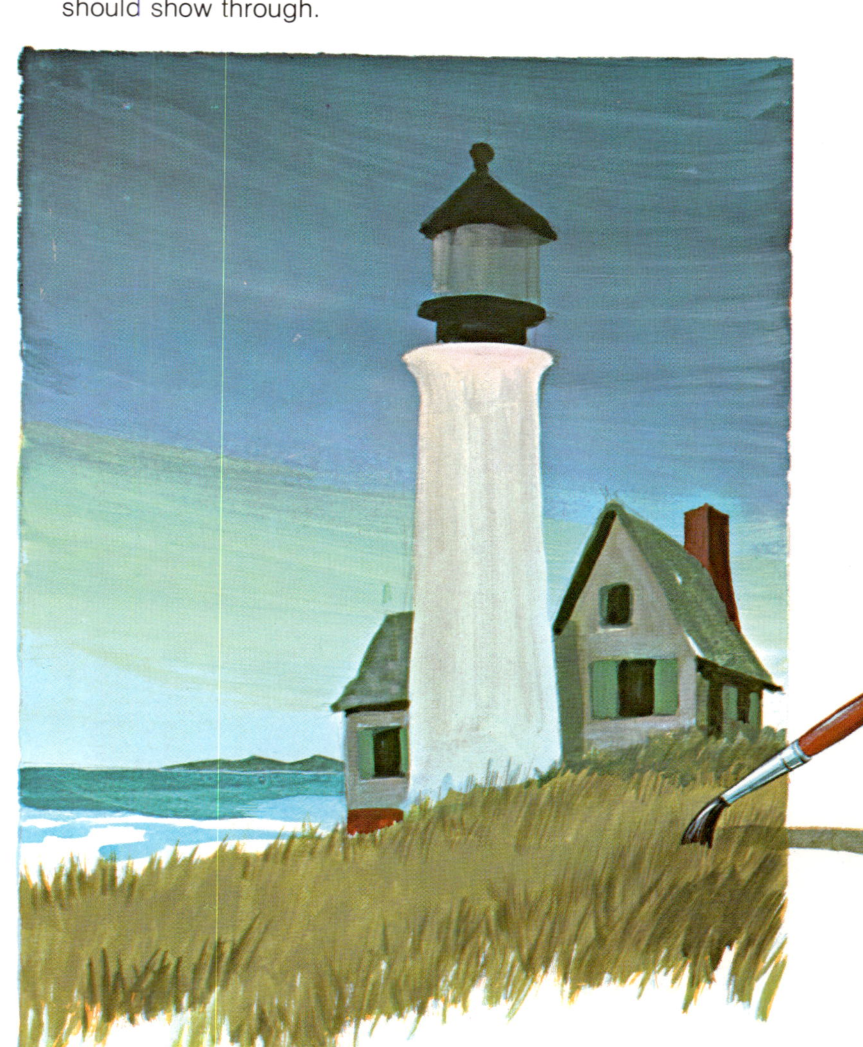

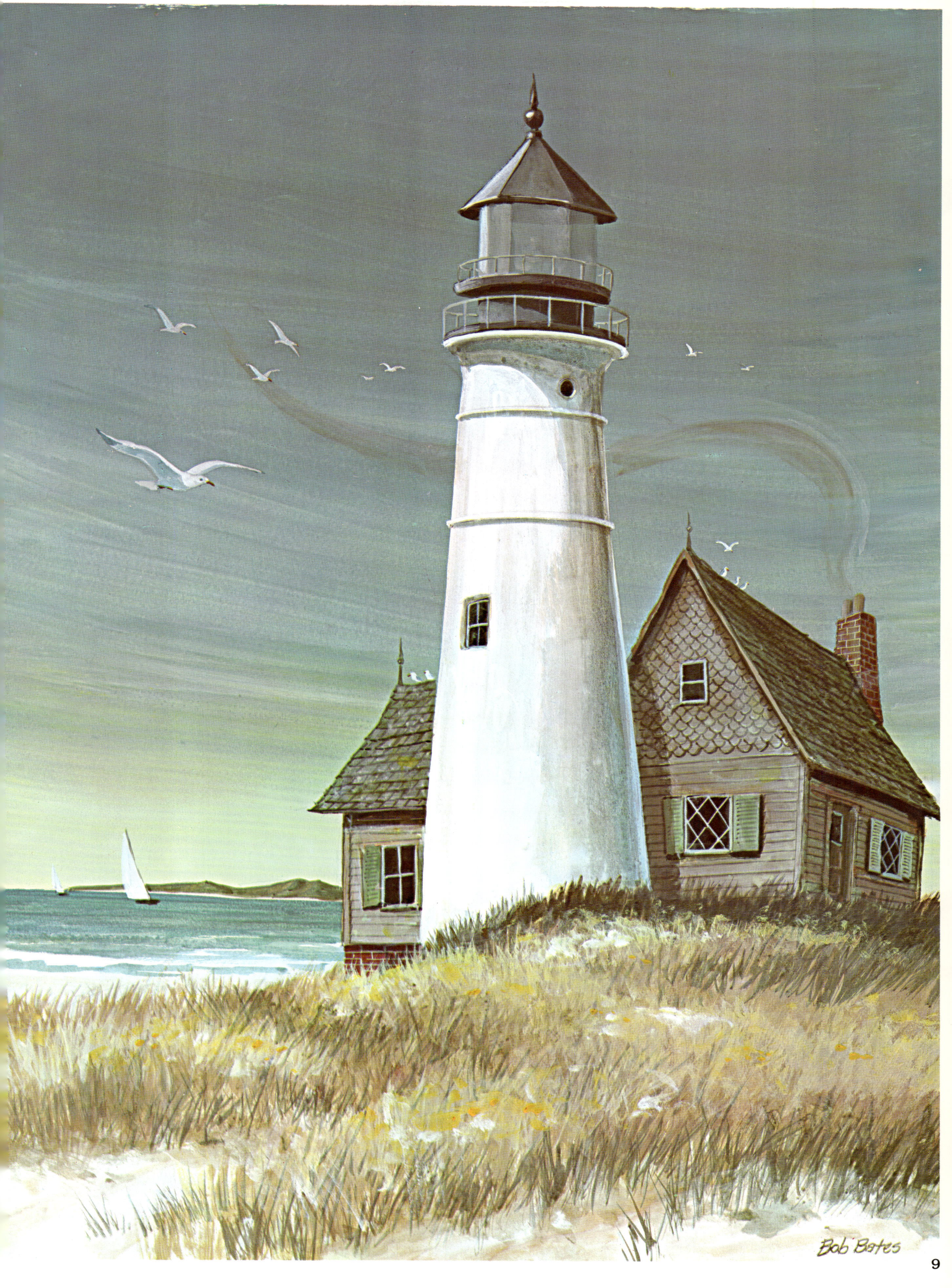
Bob Bates

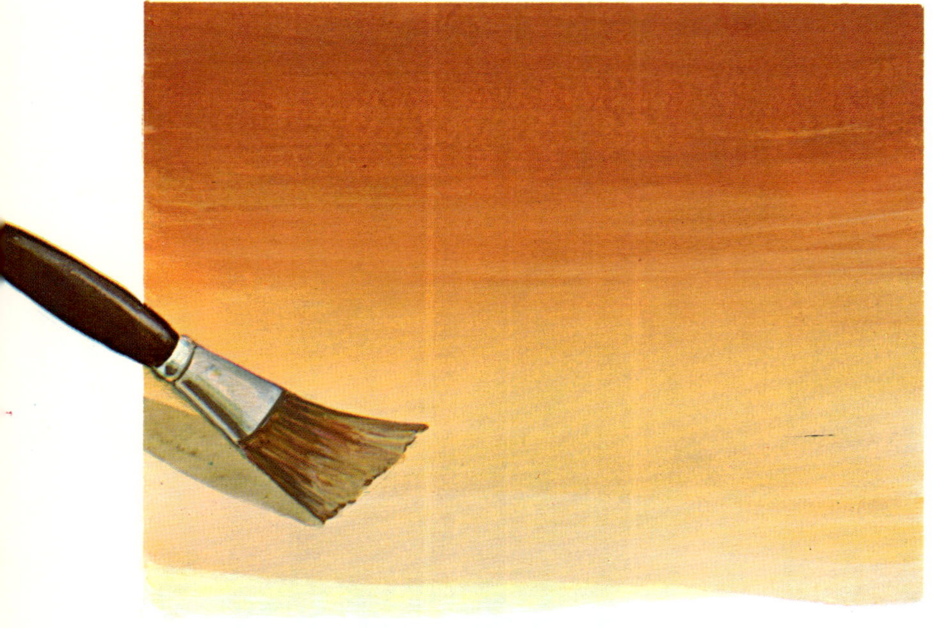

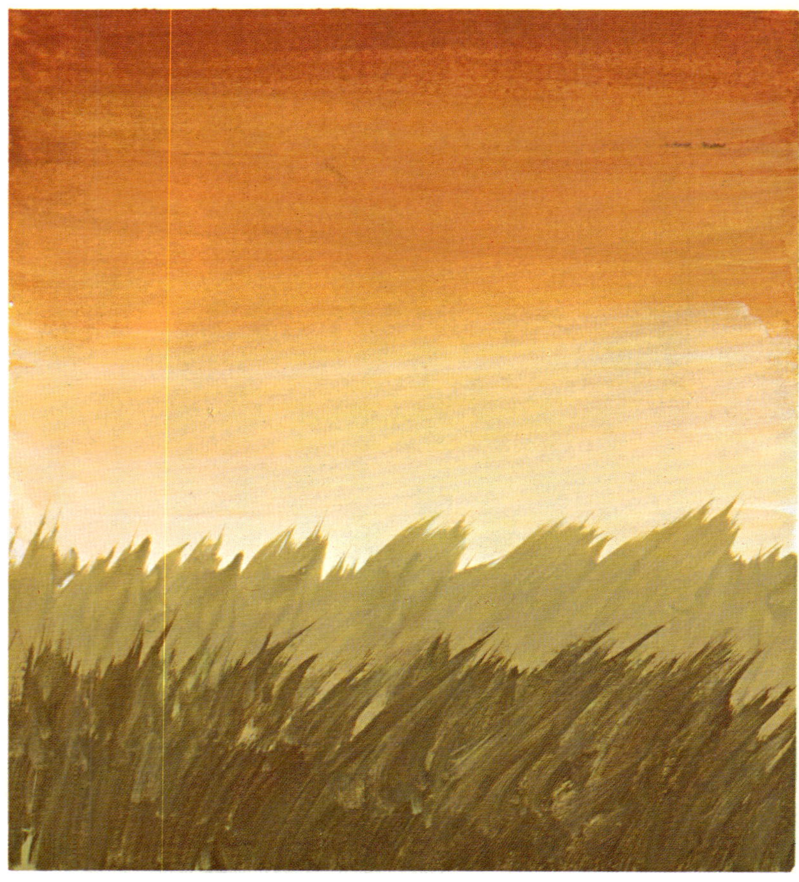

EARLY MARCH

This 1″ broad flat brush is best for your background skies.

I like to paint some dark color at the top and then some White and Ochre across the bottom and just start working the two colors into each other.

Back stroke two layers of foreground under painting of weeds. The dark foreground will tend to frame your picture and give depth to your subject. Now work the weeds in together. Don't be afraid to use many different colors in your weeds.

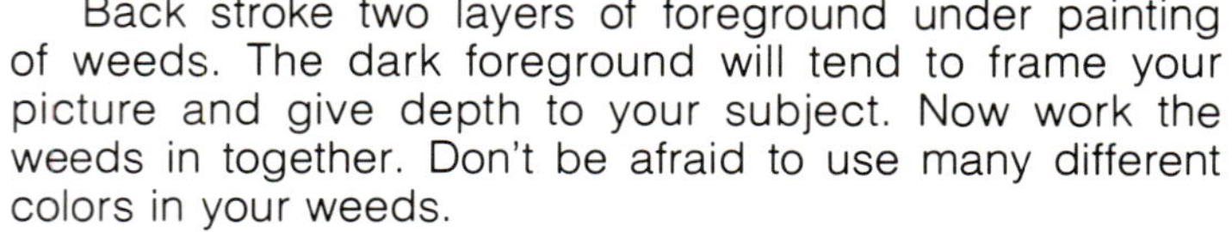

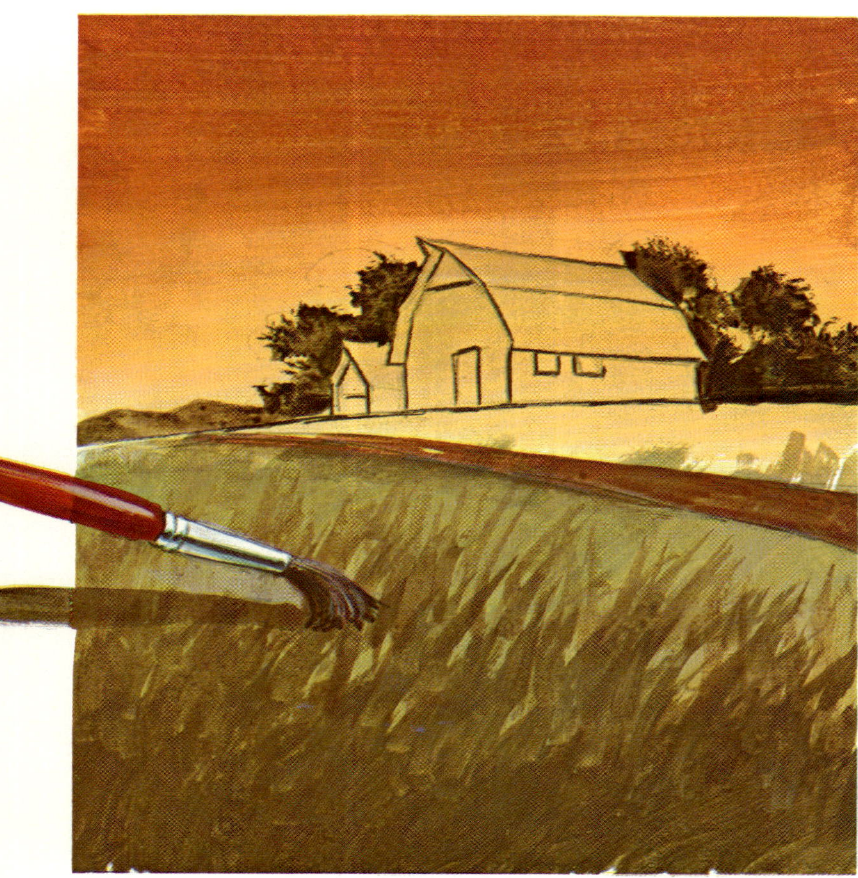

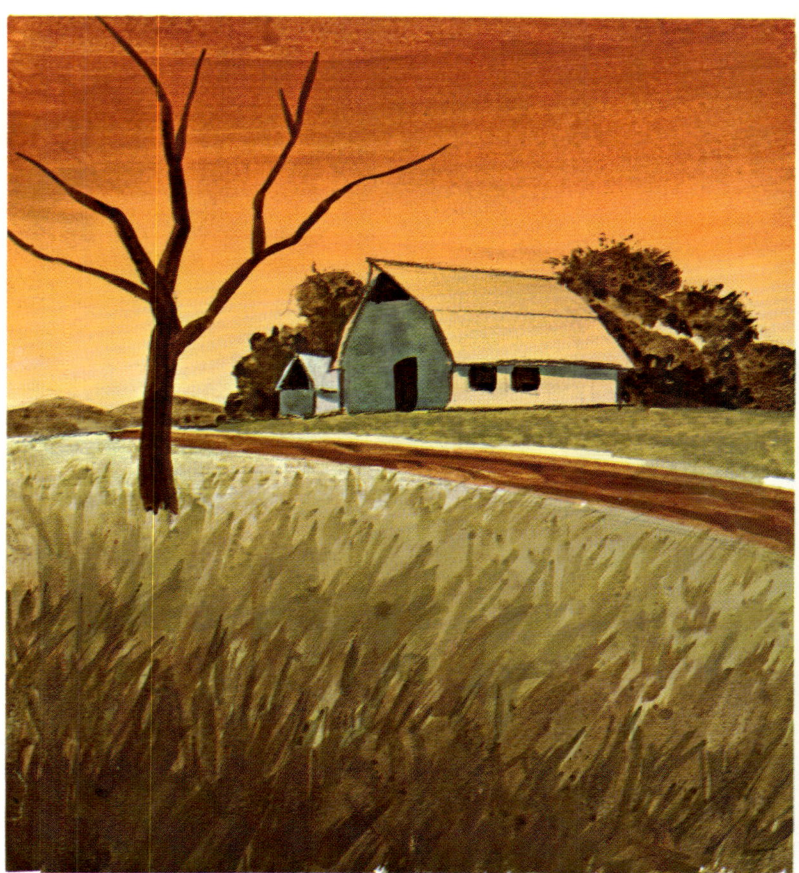

Using an old #9 brush, backstroke your foreground weeds. The trees in the background are Indo Orange, Chrome Green, Burnt Umber and Black backstroked.

You can see how important your source of light is even at this point. The dark side of the barn and under the eves all give a third dimensional effect and the contrast gives your picture interest.

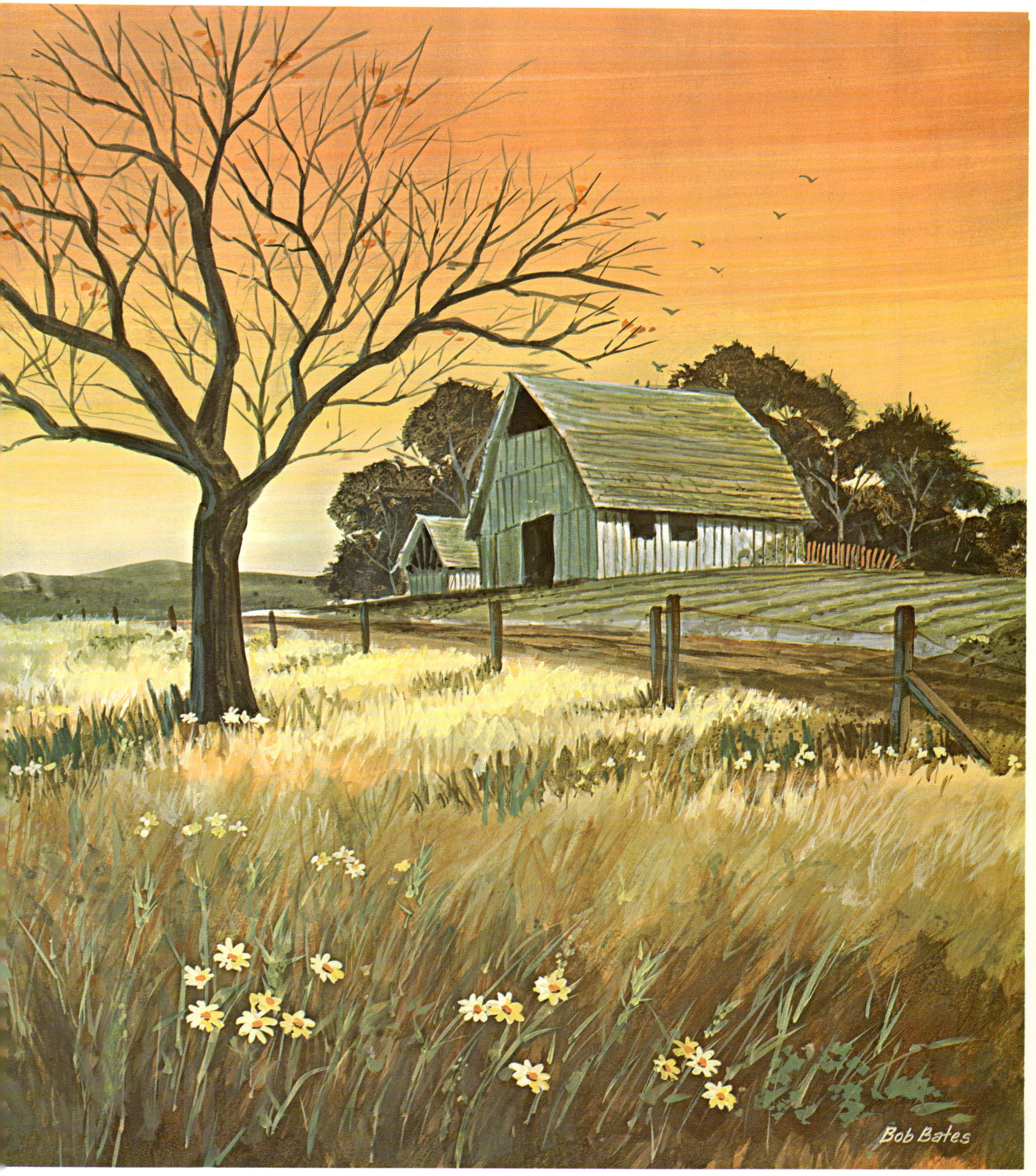

The bare tree, painted from the trunk up, is like a river with small tributaries flowing into it. Paint some of your branches on top and across others for that third dimension effect. With a #2 pointed brush paint toward the thin tops.

The white daisies in the foreground over the dark weeds add life to country paintings. These flowers seem to have become a trademark of mine through the years.

I have kept this scene simple; you may want to add some object, person, wagon, etc., to the foreground.

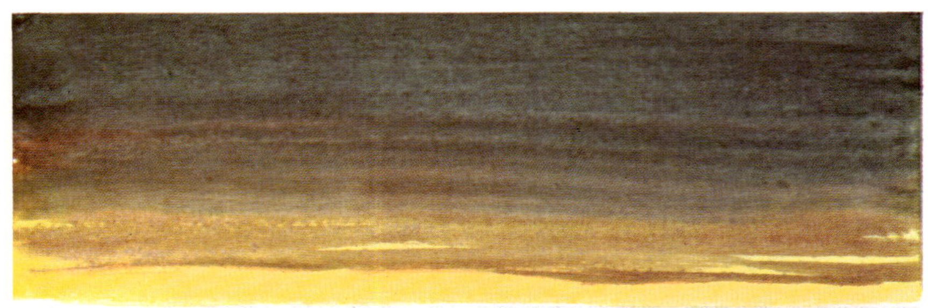

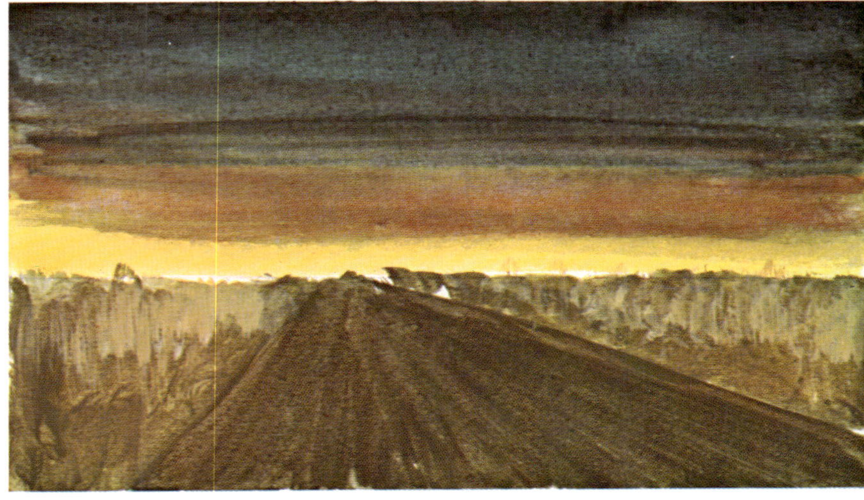

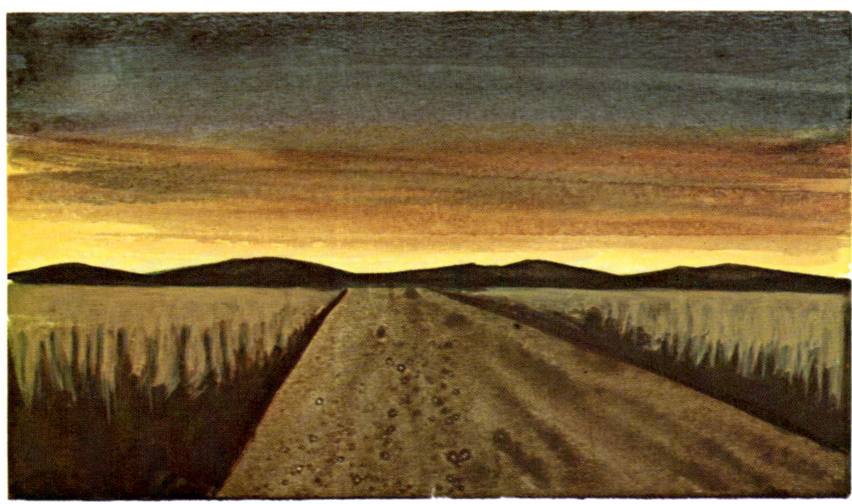

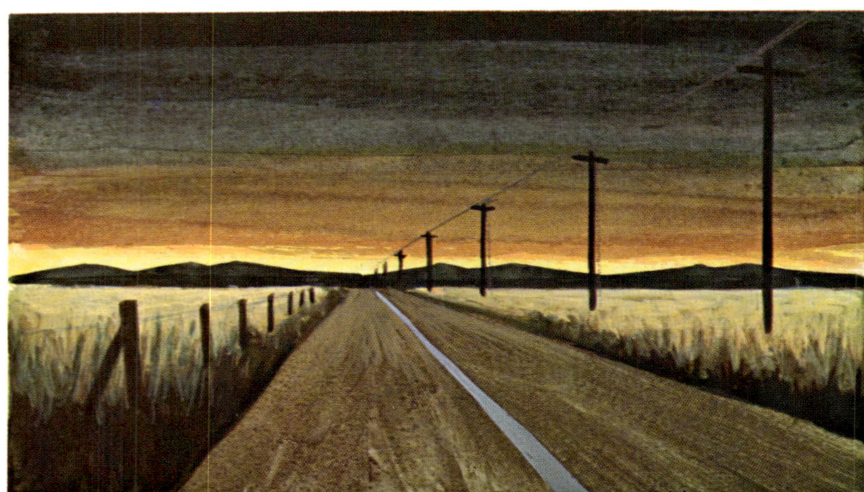

APPROACHING NIGHT

Let's have some fun with single-point perspective. You may want to try this in pencil first. If you draw thin mountains on the horizon you will get a feeling of distance. Now make them larger. See how close they suddenly become?

Painting a sunset, from light to dark also gives depth to a painting.

Semi-darkness is the feeling here and the lights in the windows of the buildings give a cozy effect.

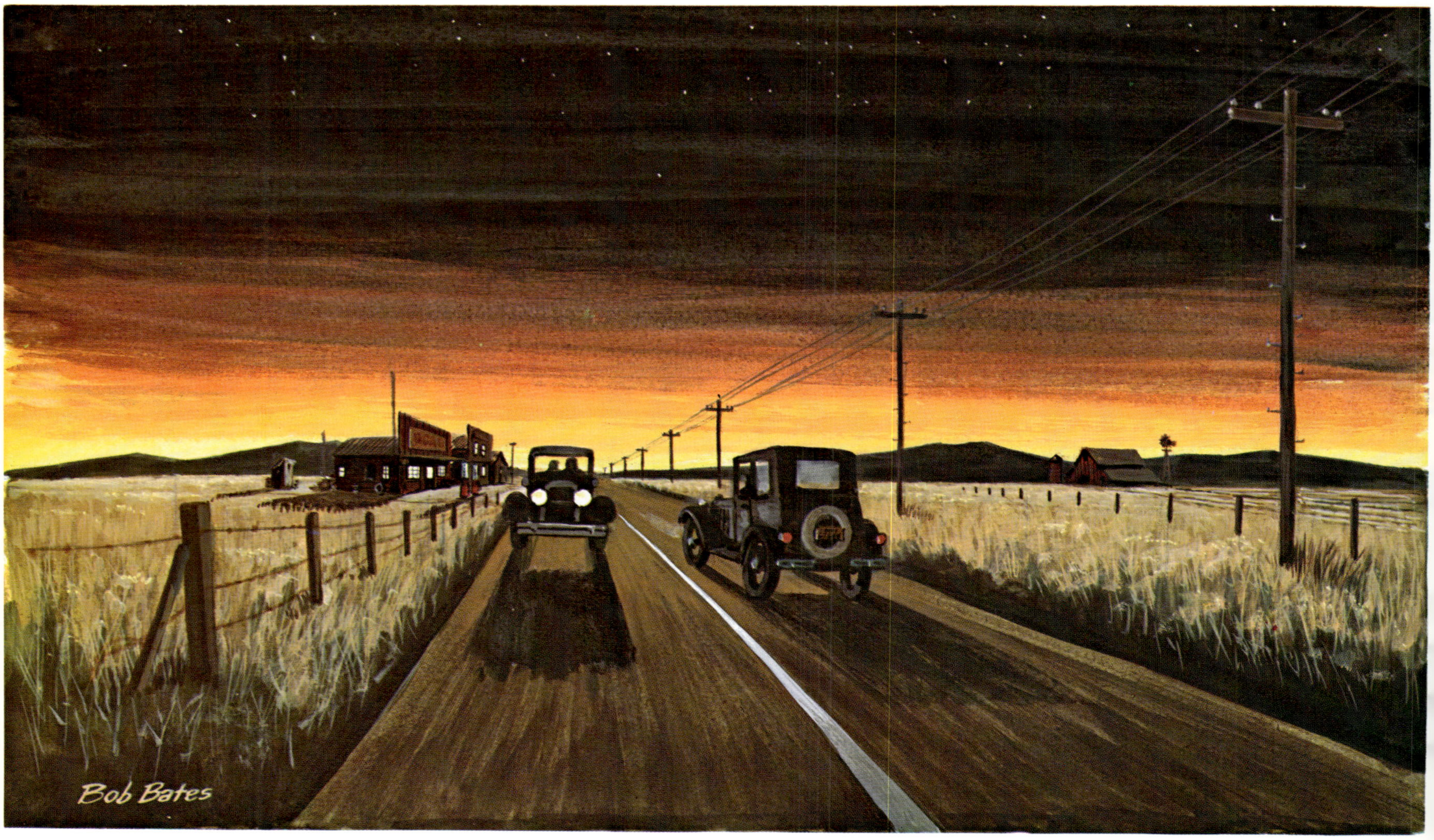

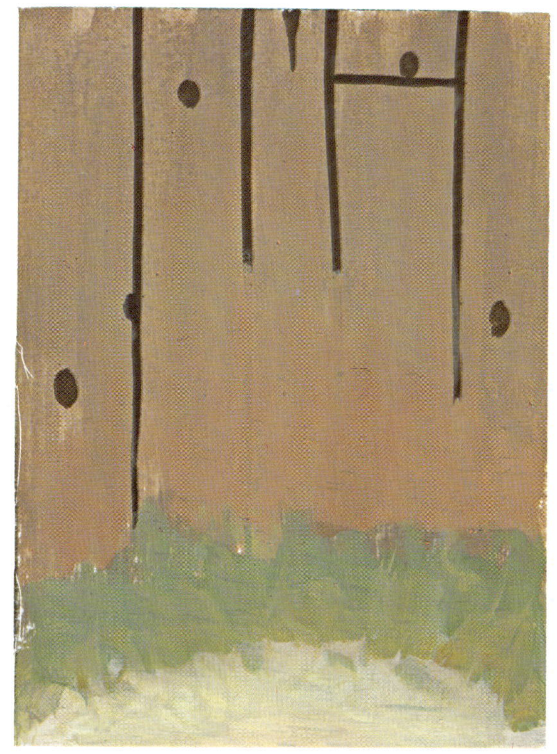

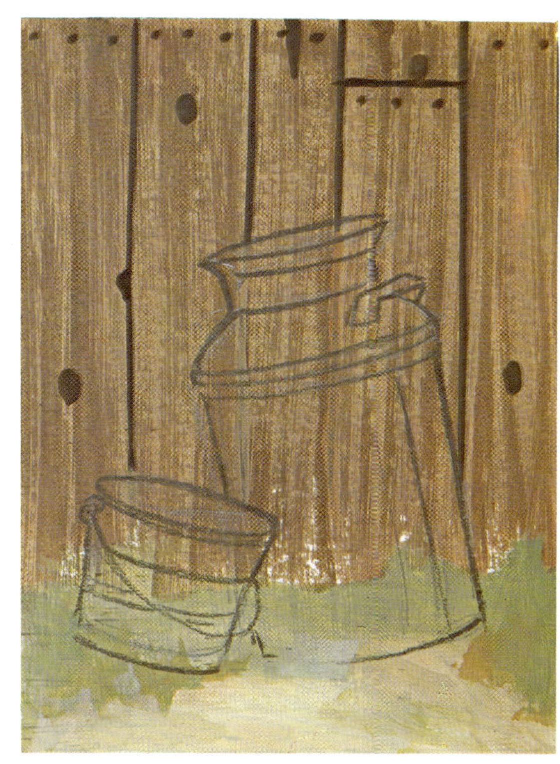

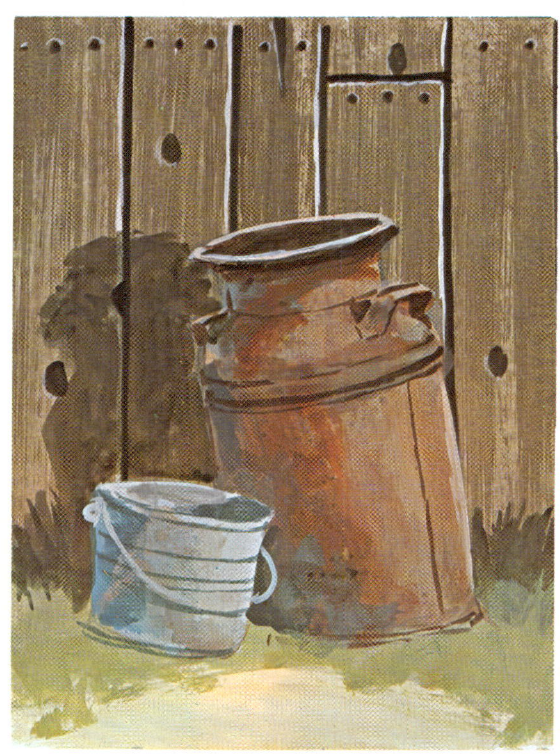

BUCKETS & WOOD SIDING

Painting wood siding can be easy to achieve. For the light wood color, use Raw Sienna, Indo Orange, Yellow and White. Black is used for knot holes and panel separations.

For grain in wood, use a dry-brush technique with darkened colors. With a #2 pointed brush you can add more details such as the nails.

Toothbrush splatter can be added as a final touch.

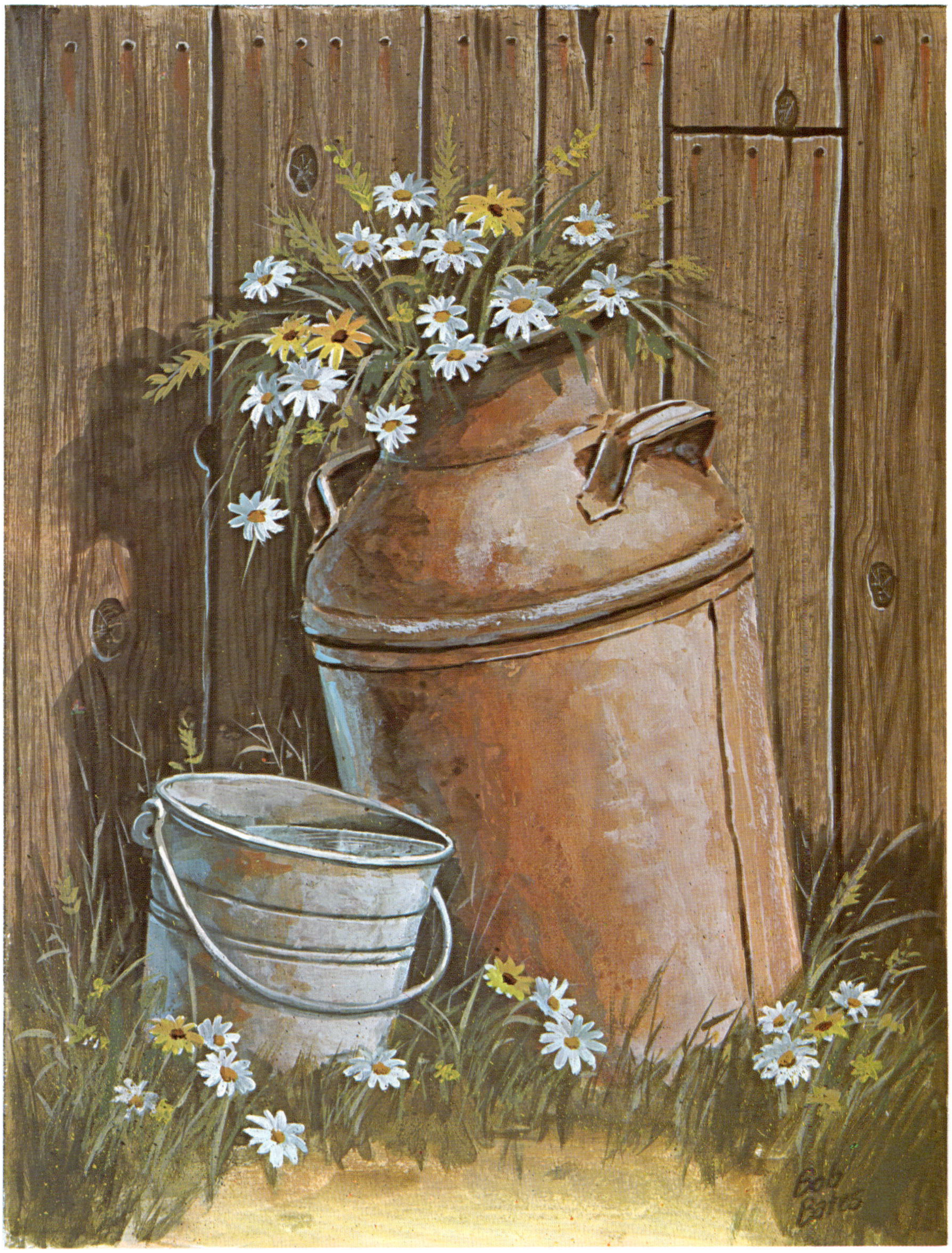

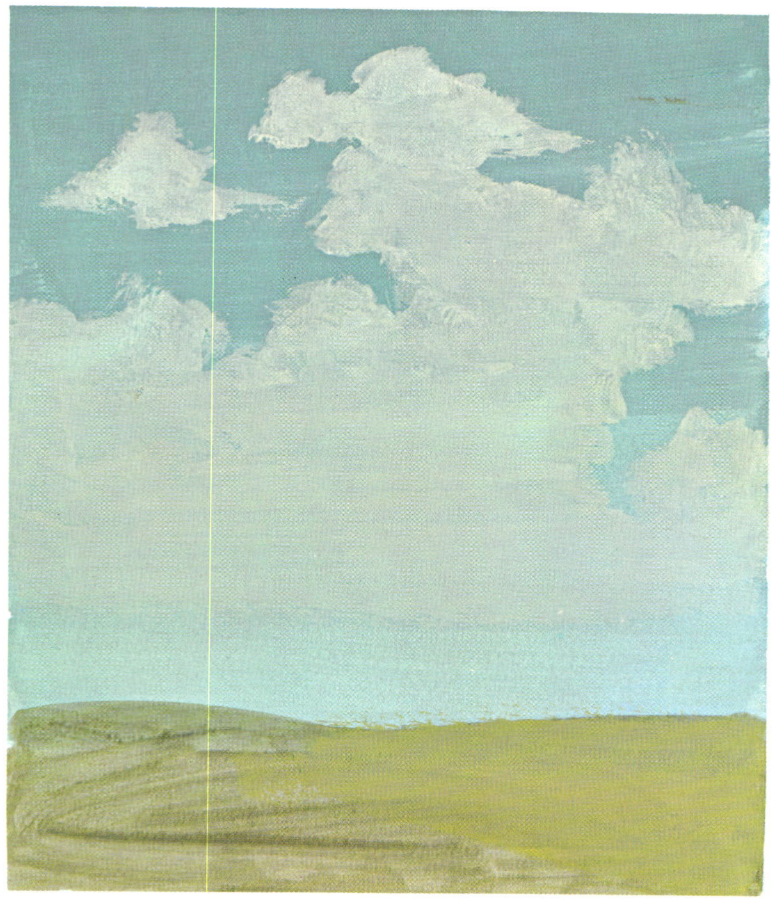
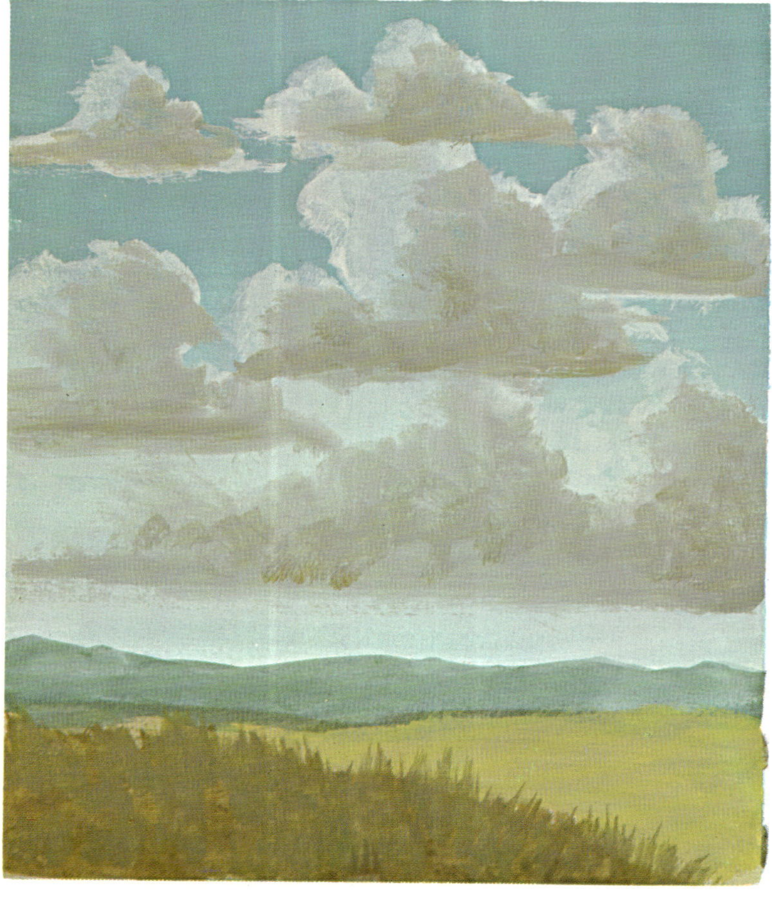
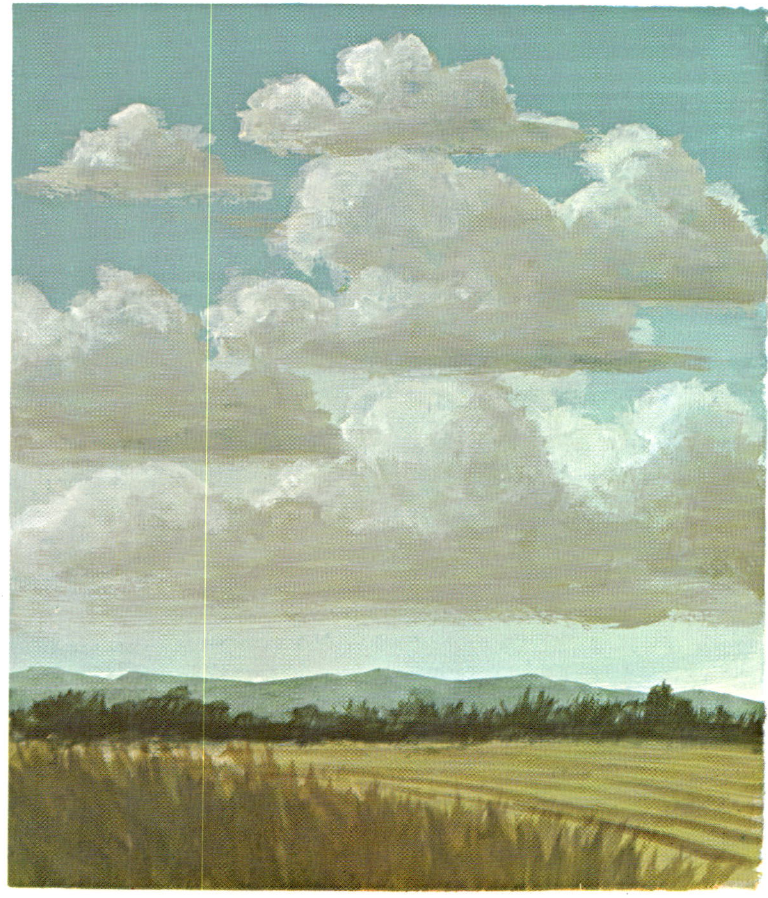

BILLOWY CLOUDS

Nothing is more beautiful than expressive clouds. In places like Arizona the clouds are unbelievable and I work my camera overtime. We are talking here about the billowy, fluffy type.

Paint your sky first using Cerulean Blue mixed with a touch of Black and a lot of White. When completely dry, add the clouds. A little blue should show through. The top of clouds are almost pure White and the roundness is achieved with darker colors such as Burnt Sienna and Indo Orange with Dark Blue.

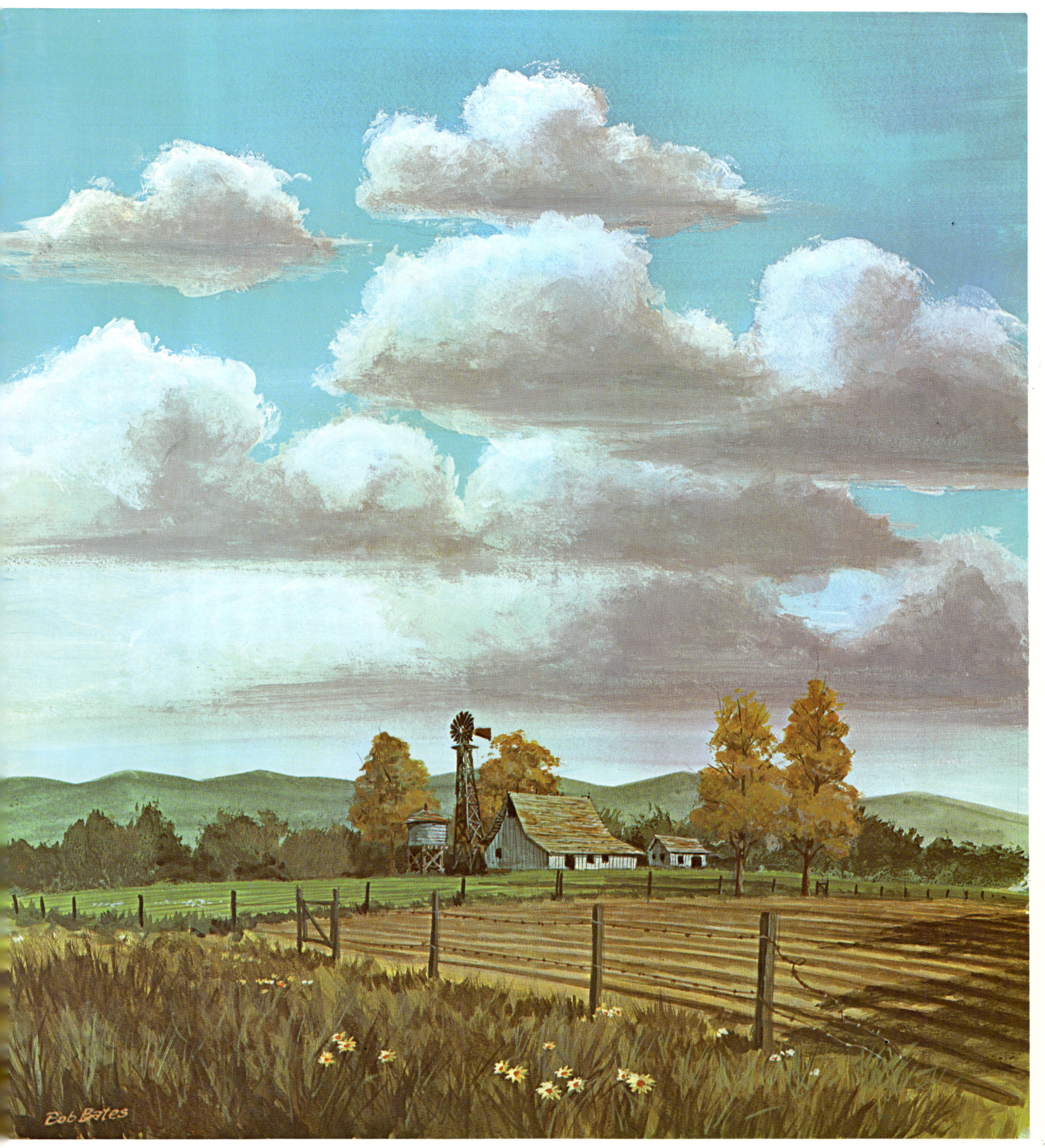

If you will look very closely you can see the wind direction in these clouds. They are puffier in the direction in which they are traveling. Again, remember your source of light and make them lighter on top. All shapes should be different.

Clouds definitely add to a painting. They set a mood, create shadows on the ground and distant hills, and are marvelous contrast.

Painting clouds at sunset can be difficult, but rewarding. Don't be afraid of bright Reds, Oranges, Yellow, Ochre, etc., on top of the deep Blue sky at the top of the picture.

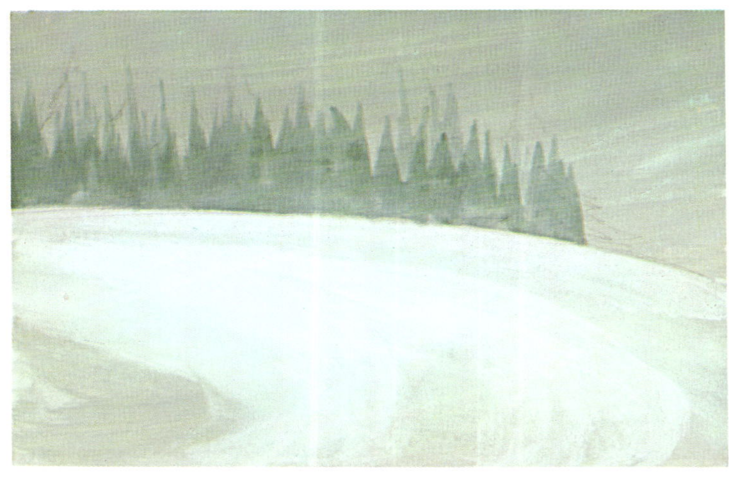

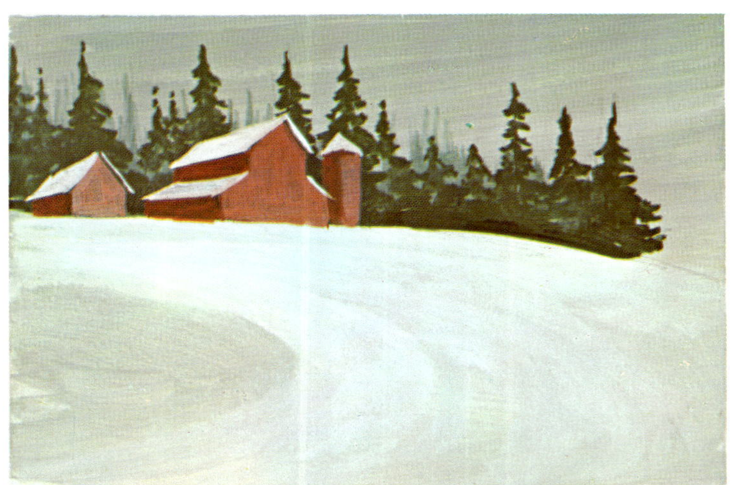

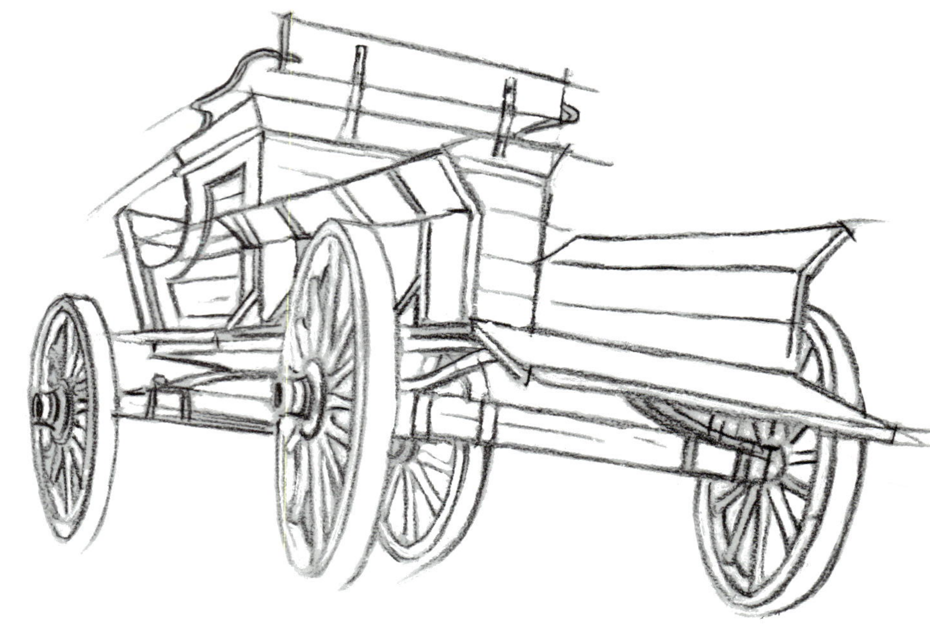

WAGON IN THE SNOW

If you are as much of a fan of the Foster Books as I am, you probably have noted entire books devoted to painting snow scenes. When I paint snow, I add White paint and Cerulean Blue. On completion, I go back and add more pure White.

Draw the wagon in detail before painting it remembering your perspective with the vanishing points.

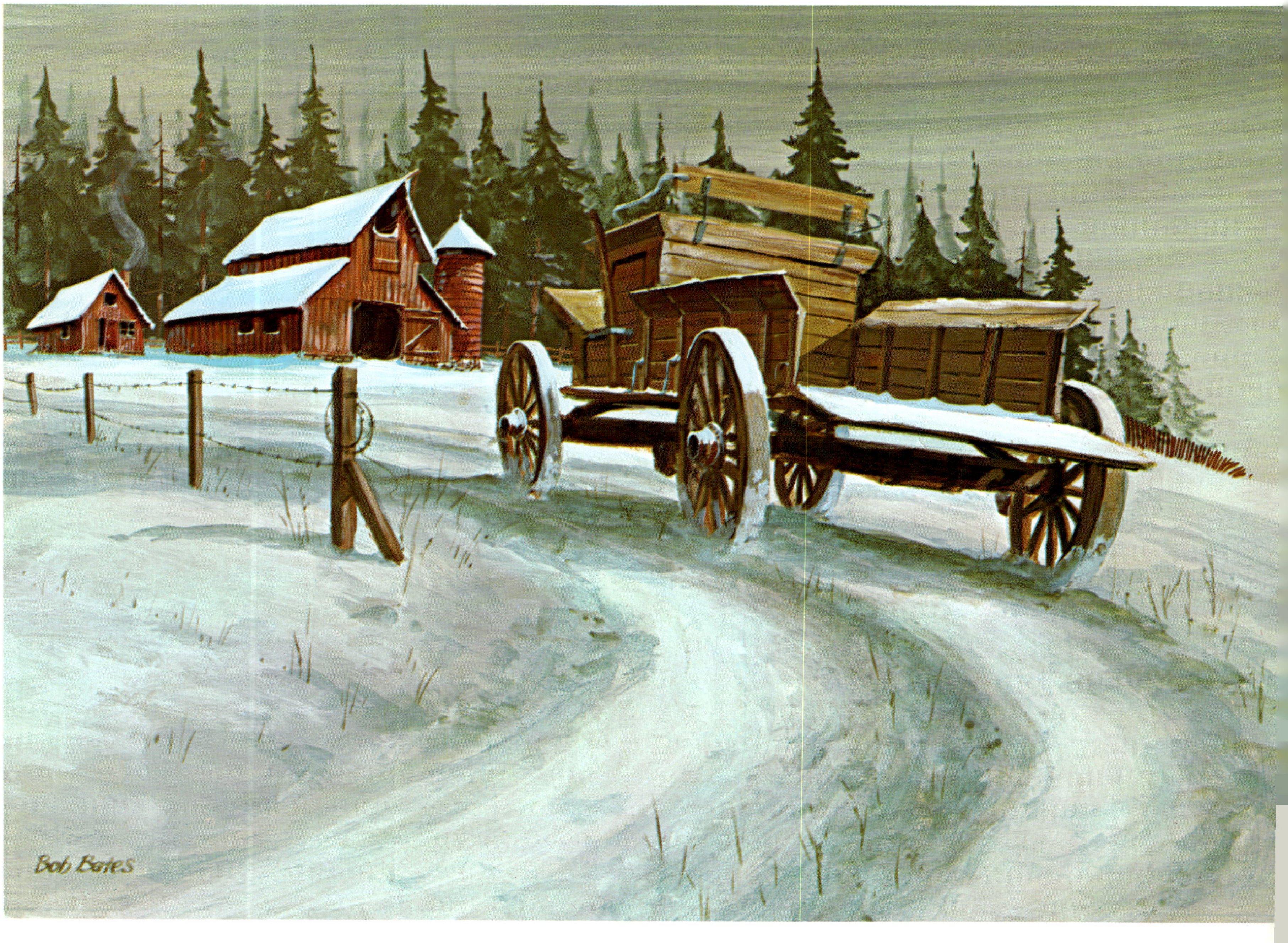

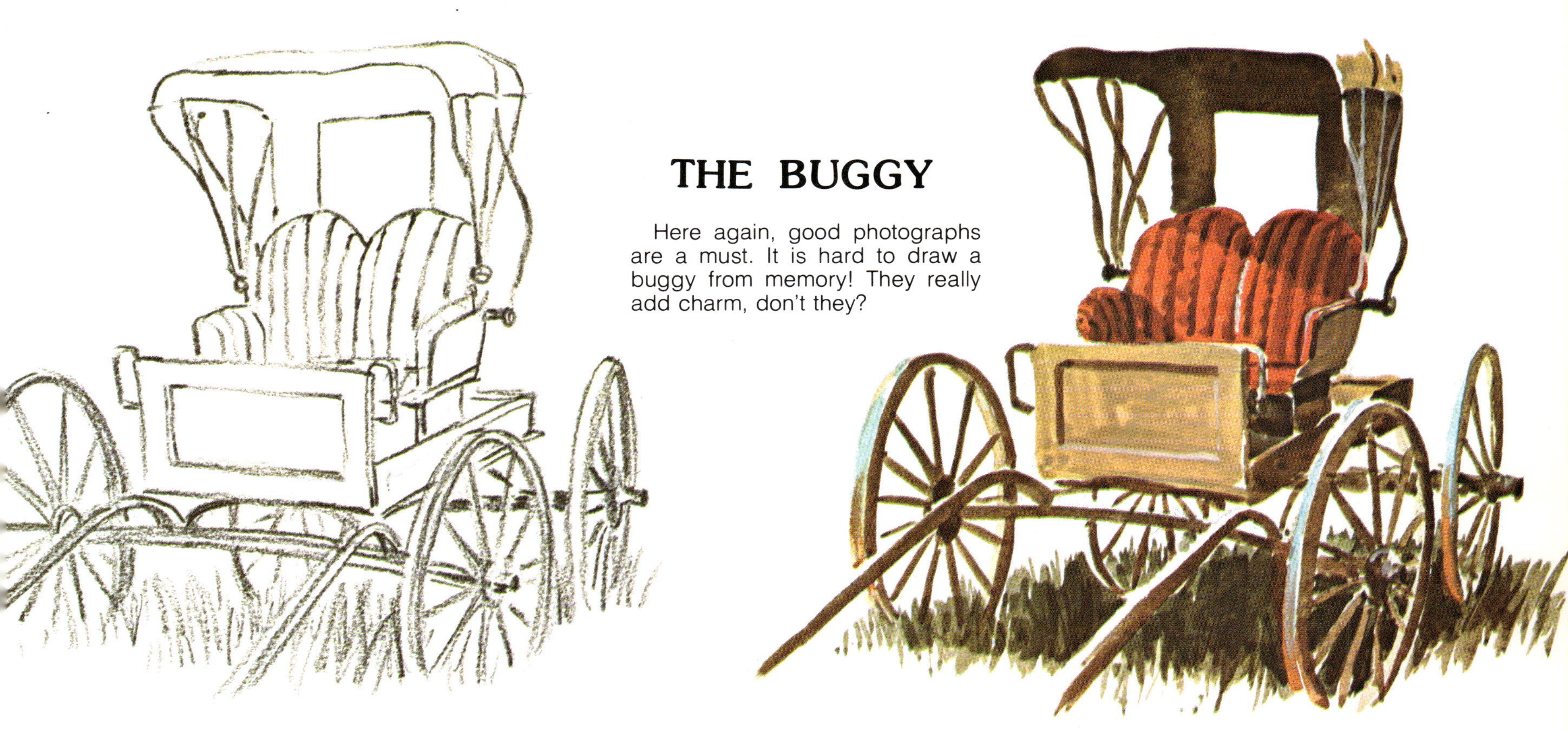

THE BUGGY

Here again, good photographs are a must. It is hard to draw a buggy from memory! They really add charm, don't they?

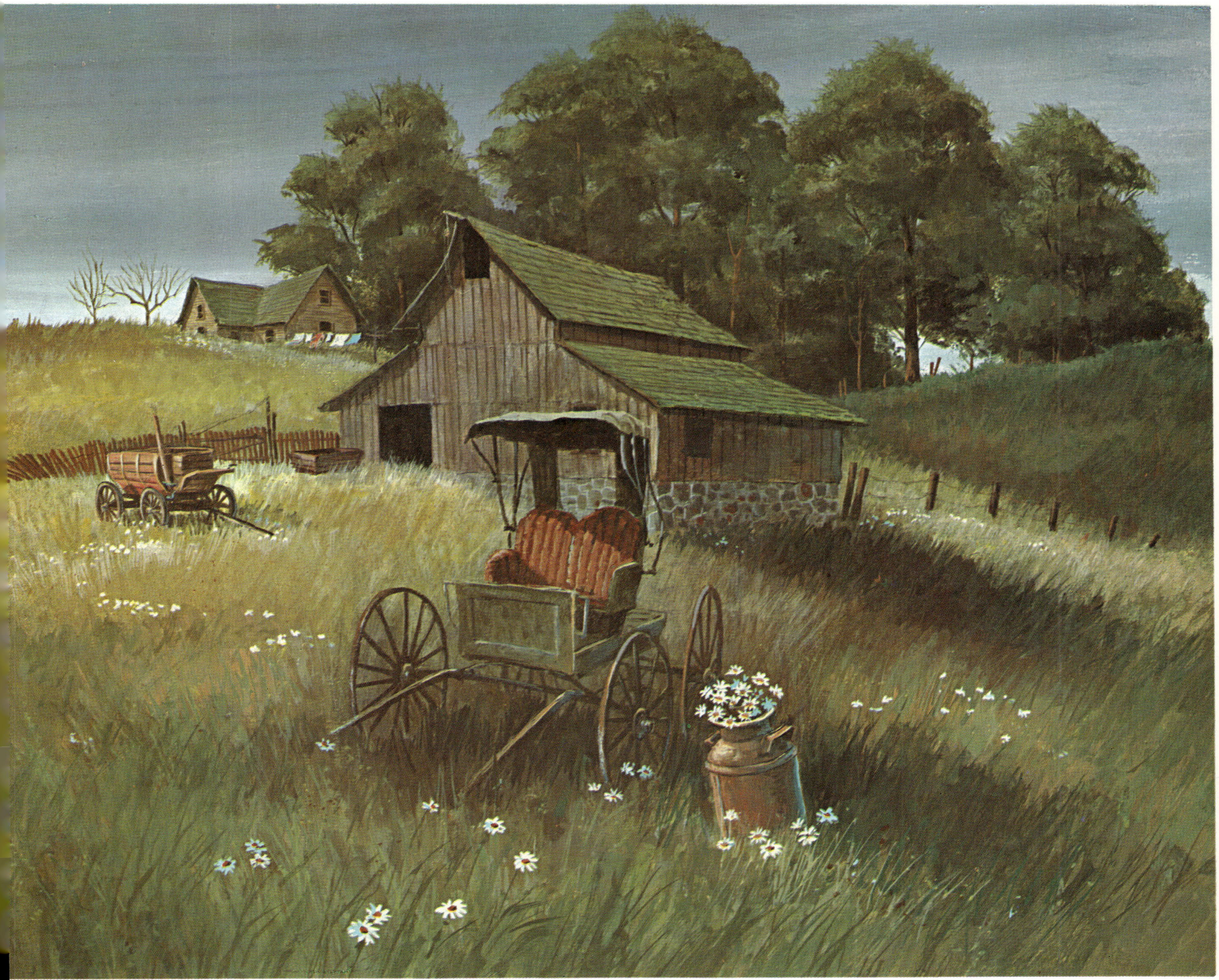

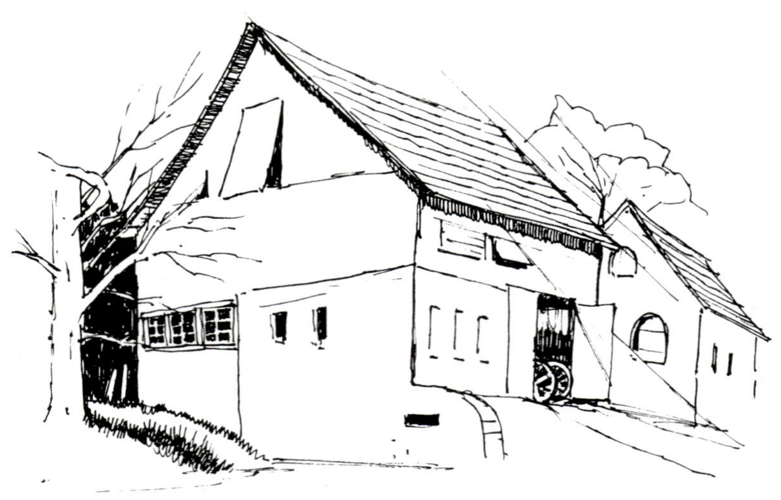

AMISH BARN

Some of the most interesting country and picturesque barns in the world are found around Lancaster, Penn. The combination of wood and stone construction is so expressive and so interesting to paint. Notice the stream running through the lower section of this barn. This cools the food stored in the mounded area which is their refrigeration. The Amish lead a very simple life.

In both this painting and the Ole' Fishing Boat, composition is triangular in shape. The "S" shape and "circular" are also popular forms of composition.

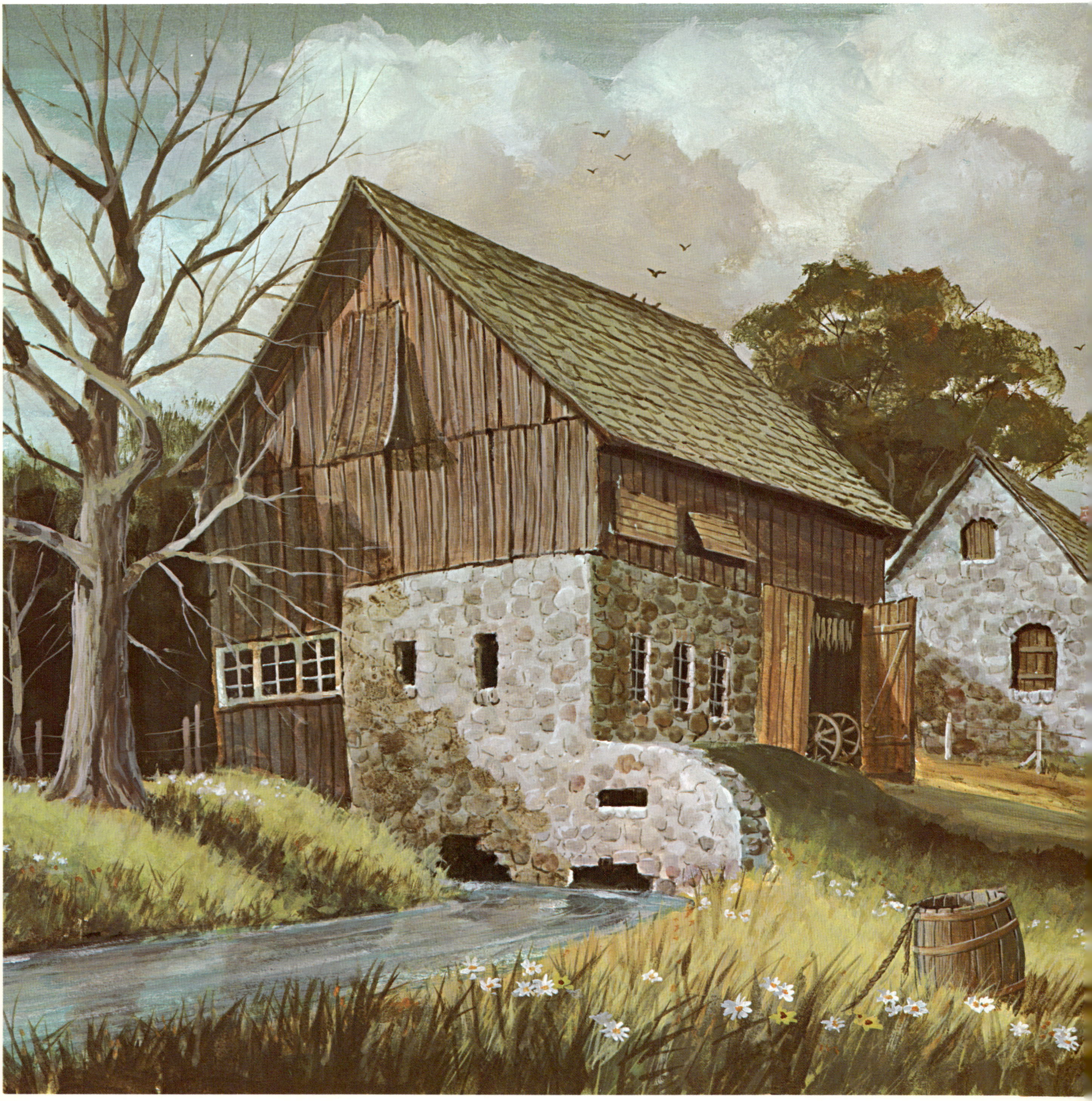

THE OLE' FISHING BOAT

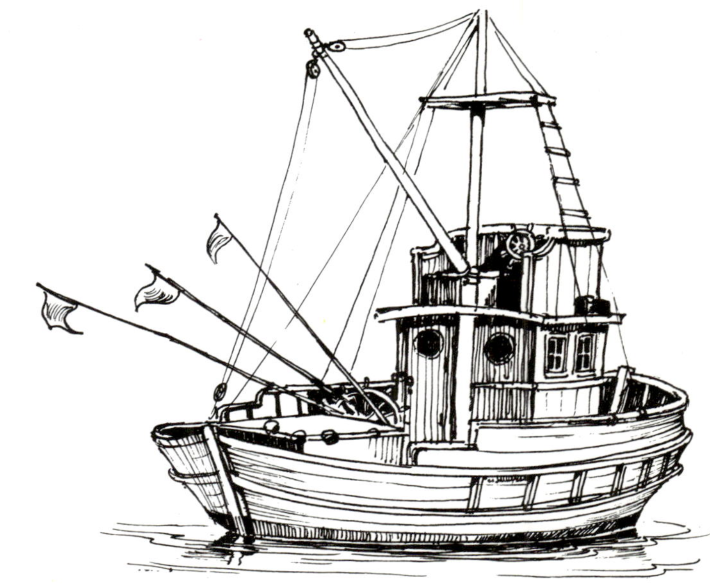

As I have said, barns are my first love and my second would have to be the old fishing boats. The harbors of Newport, Santa Barbara and San Diego, Calif. are great for painting these picturesque scenes.

Here again, practice sketching first. Keep the bow and stern lined up so that the cabin will remain centered.

Reflections in the water are straight under the object. Paint the water a dirty blue-green. As you paint the boat, add a glaze of each color in the water below for your reflection.

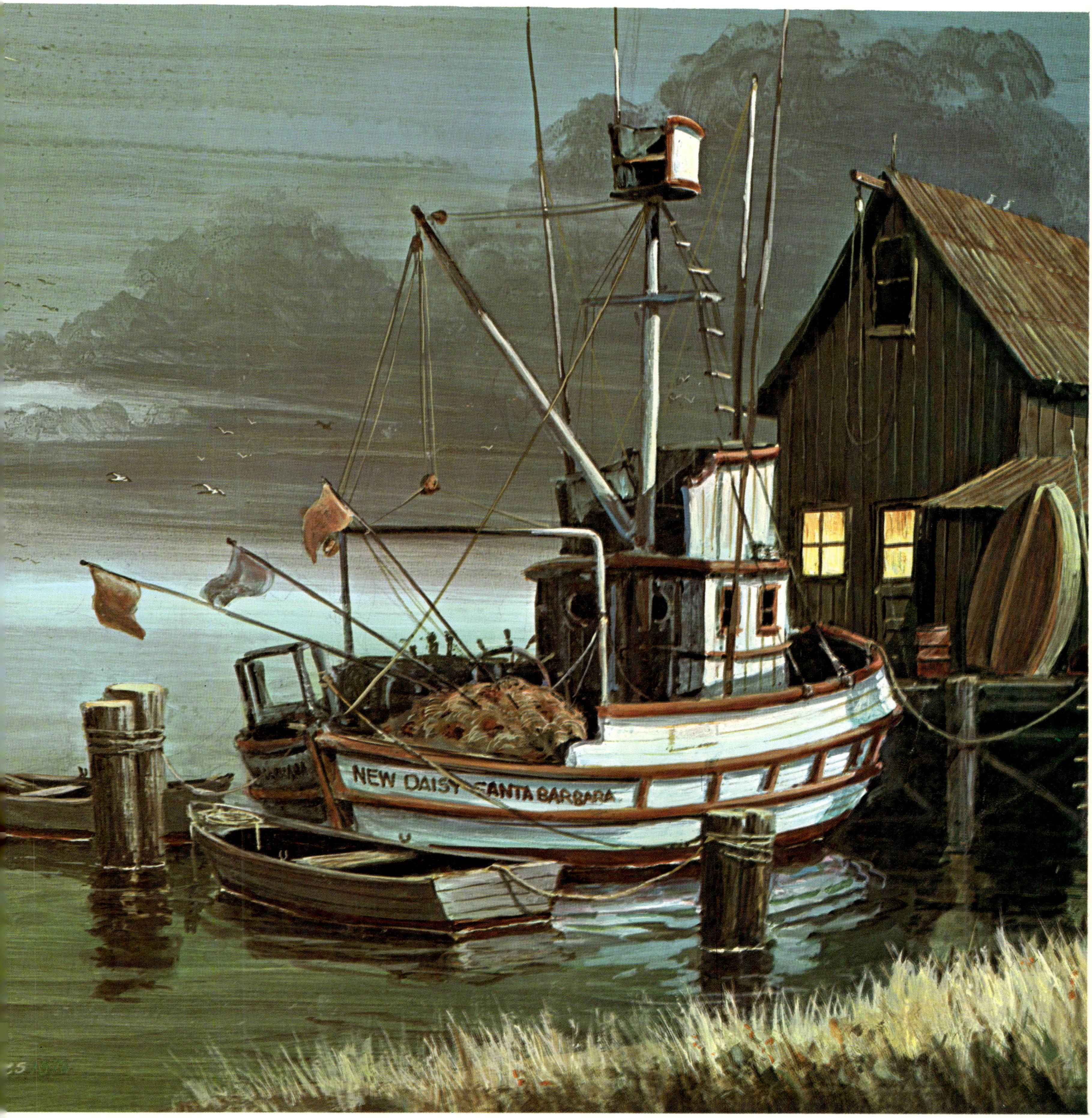

IN-COMING FOG

Here is a case of artist's license. The seagull is a resident of Balboa, Calif. and the boat was found off Cape Cod.

Let's try water color technique here. Start with a wet board. On your palette mix Black, Ochre, Blue, and Green. Keep the paints wet and build up the color until you get the desired depth. The bird is painted in White with Black and Gray details.

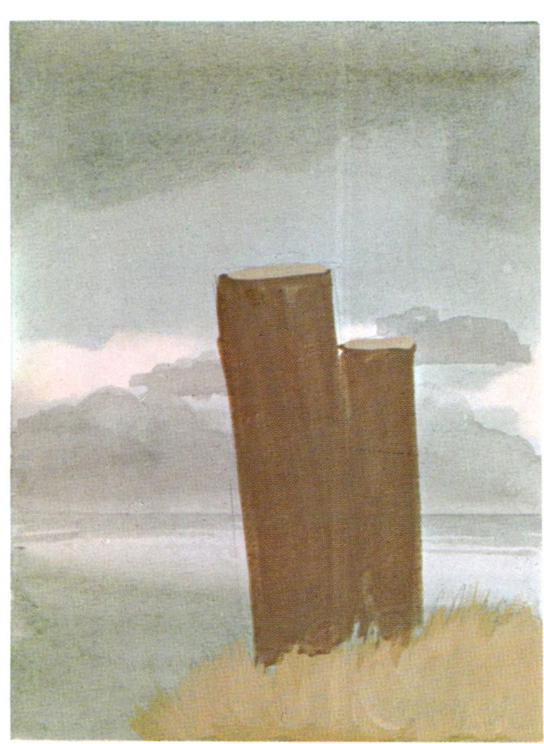

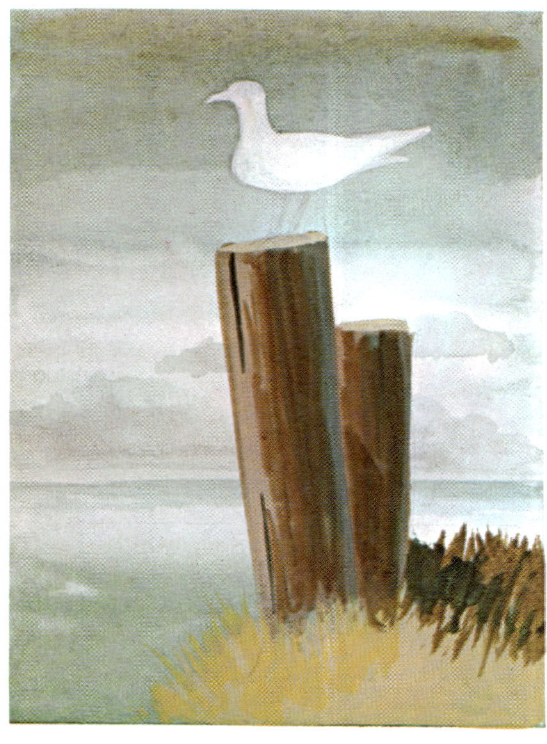

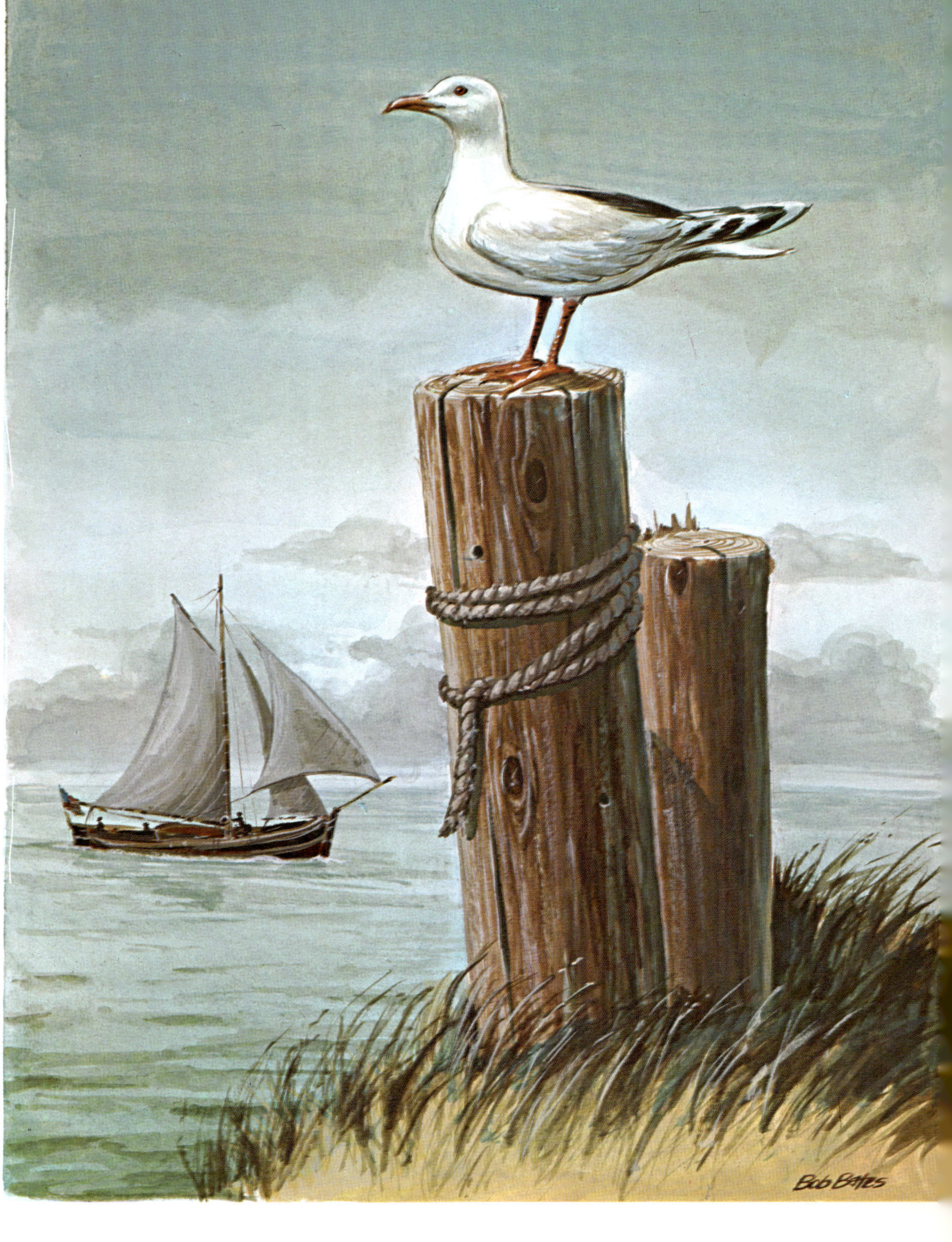

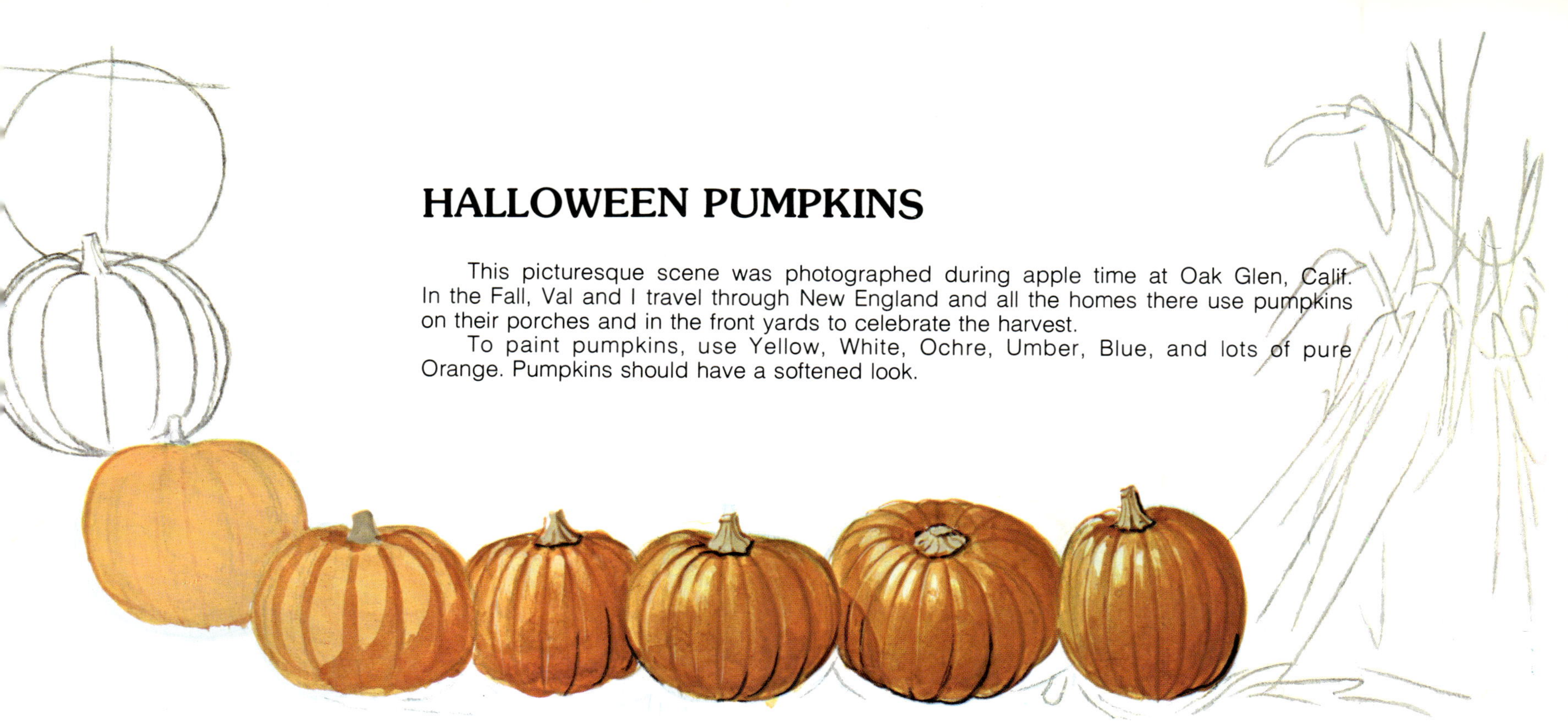

HALLOWEEN PUMPKINS

This picturesque scene was photographed during apple time at Oak Glen, Calif. In the Fall, Val and I travel through New England and all the homes there use pumpkins on their porches and in the front yards to celebrate the harvest.

To paint pumpkins, use Yellow, White, Ochre, Umber, Blue, and lots of pure Orange. Pumpkins should have a softened look.

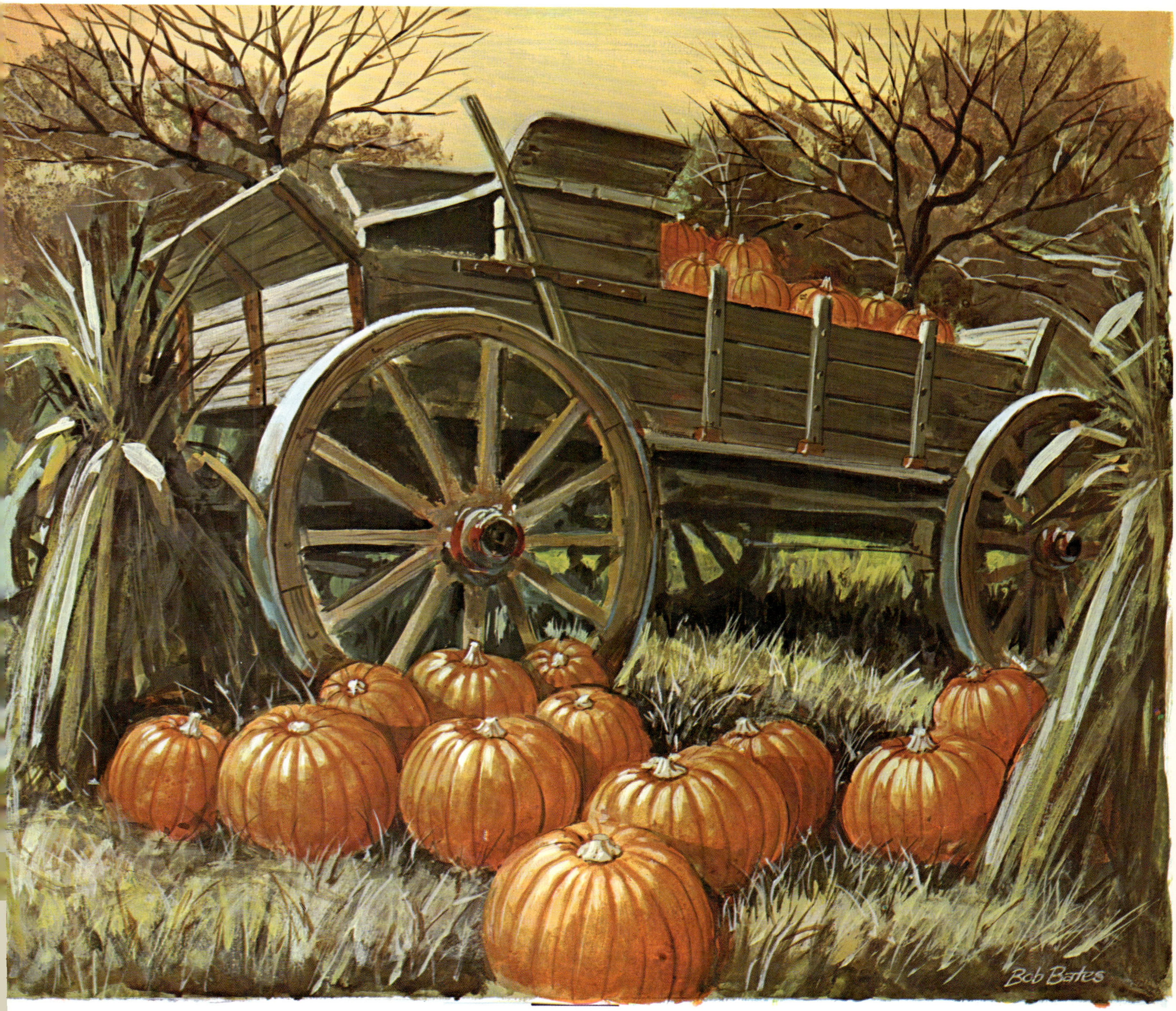

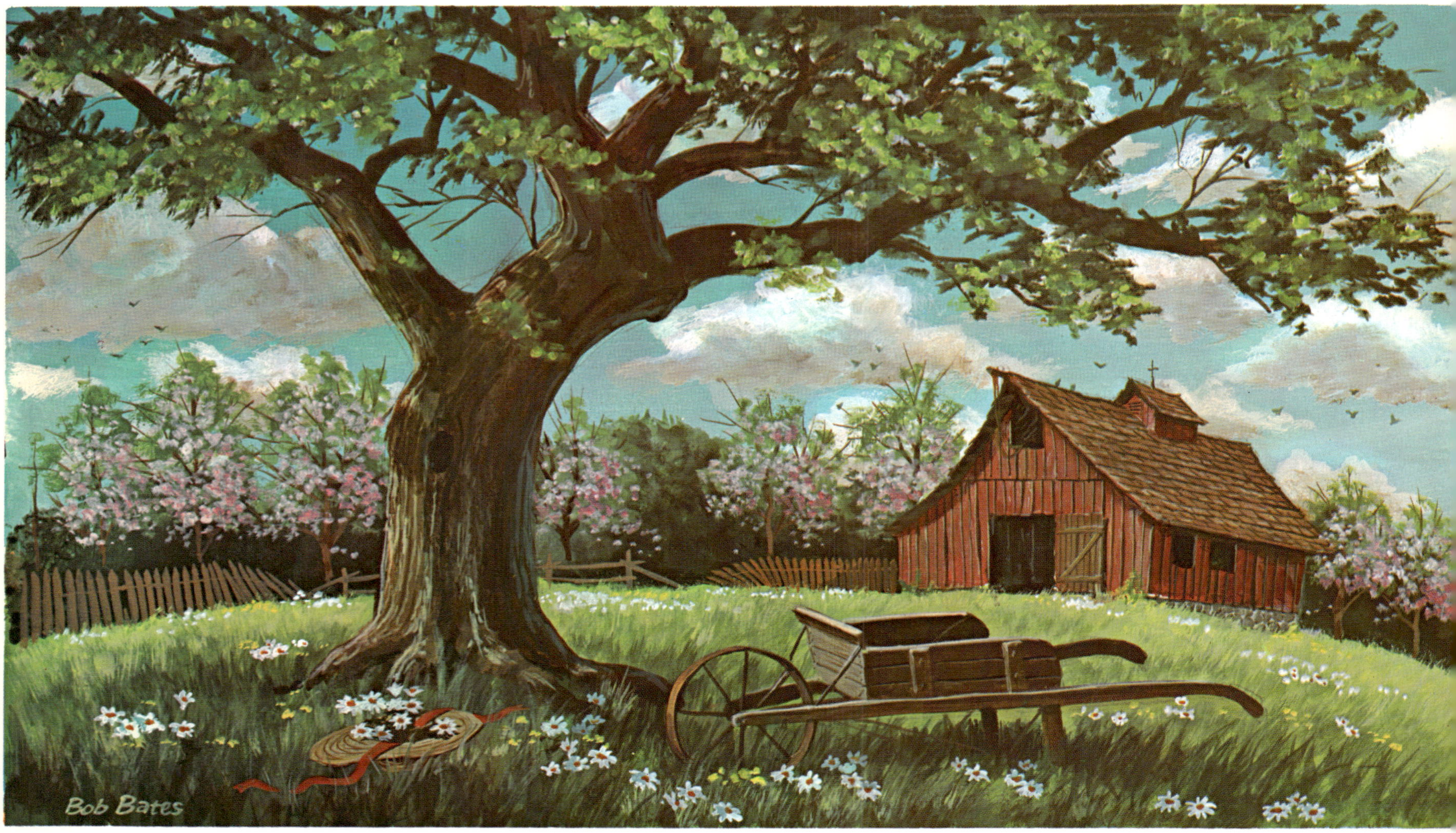

Bob Bates

SPRING

Here we have free use of Yellow, Light Green, bright colors and strong Whites for your blossoms, flowers, and clouds. You will notice I do not put people in my paintings—however—a young lady has obviously been here.

SUMMER

Spring blossoms have gone, it's warm now and someone has hung up the swing. The blue-green shade gives a cooling effect. Cast lots of shadows on the tree trunks.

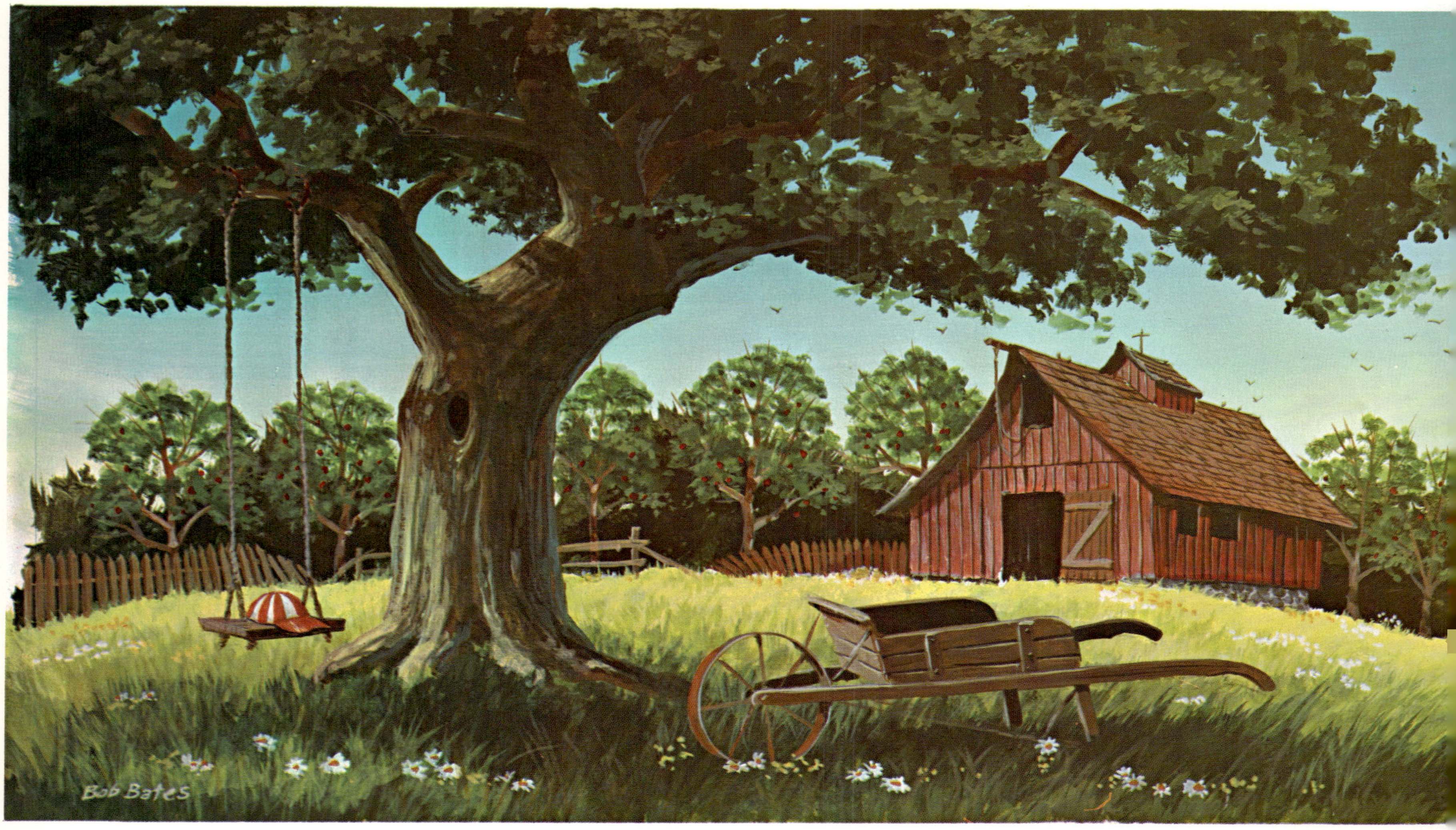

Bob Bates

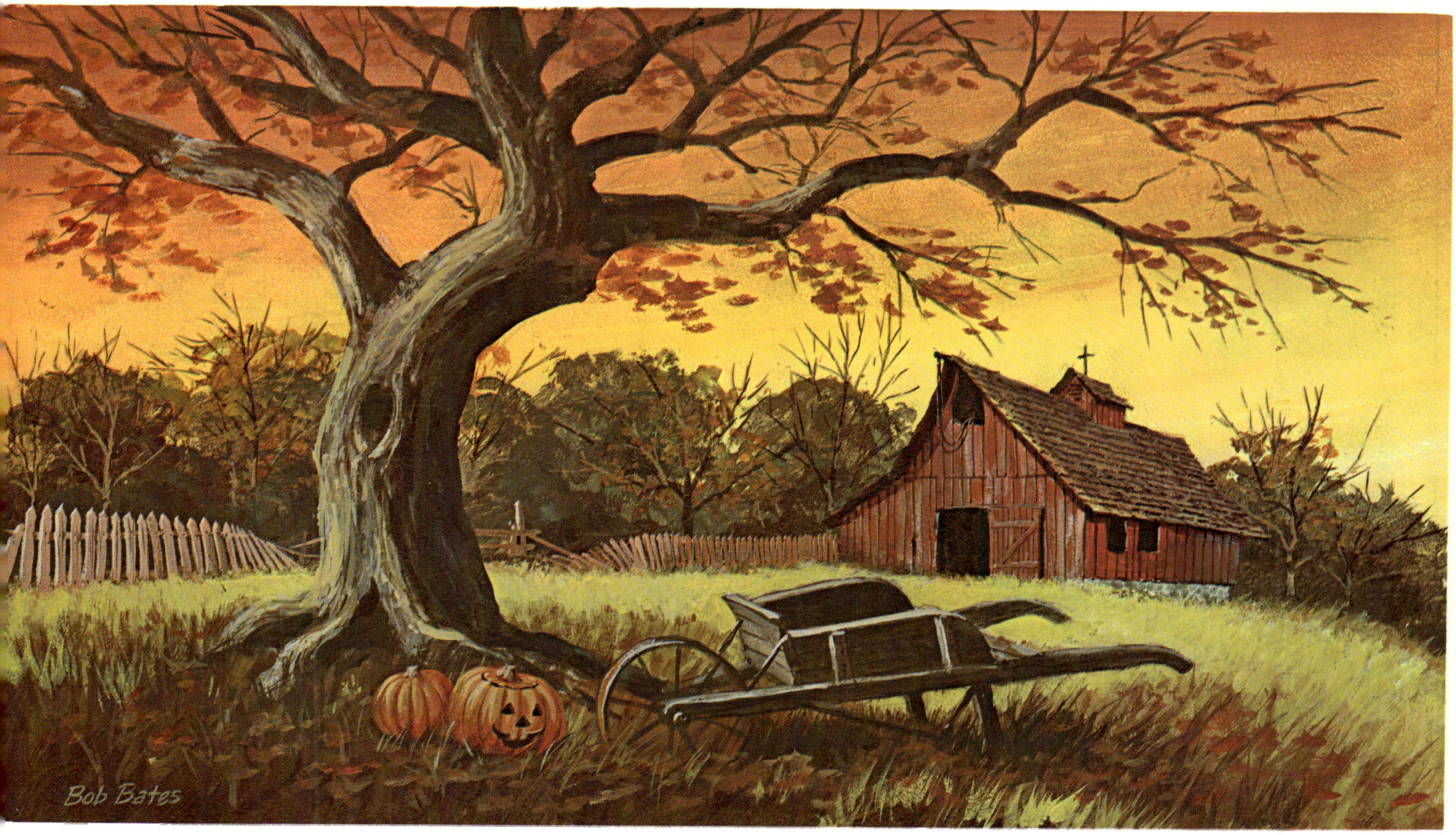

FALL

Fall in New England is breath-taking. Use your raw Orange, Yellow and Ochre on the background trees and raw, bright, red-orange and Sienna for remaining leaves on foreground tree. Time to carve the pumpkin.

WINTER

We travel again to enjoy the snow in our mountains as it doesn't snow too often in Whittier! I love to paint the snow on trees. When the wind blows, the snow sticks to one side of the tree. Use blue glaze for snow shadows. Check the antique wooden skates!

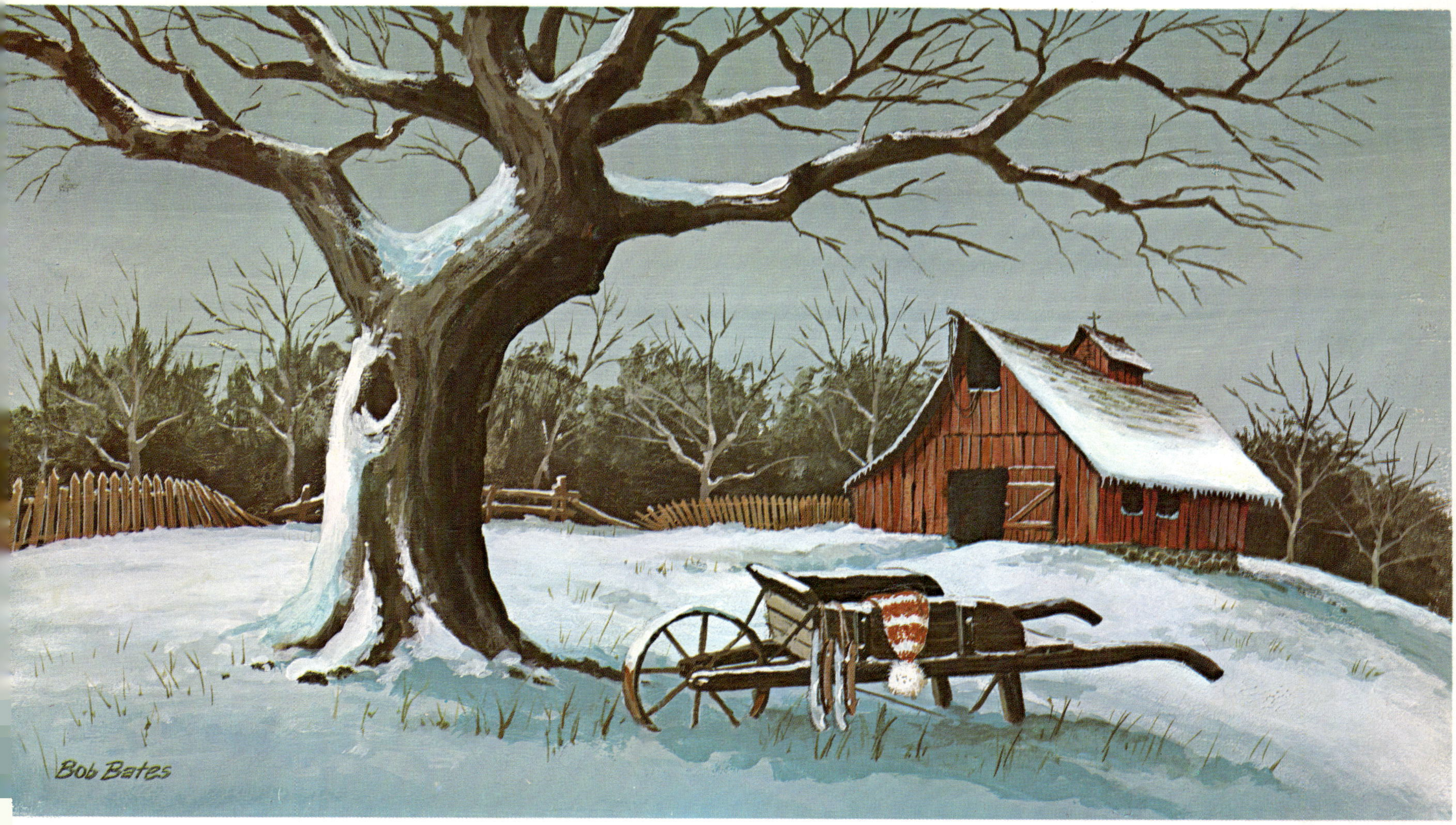

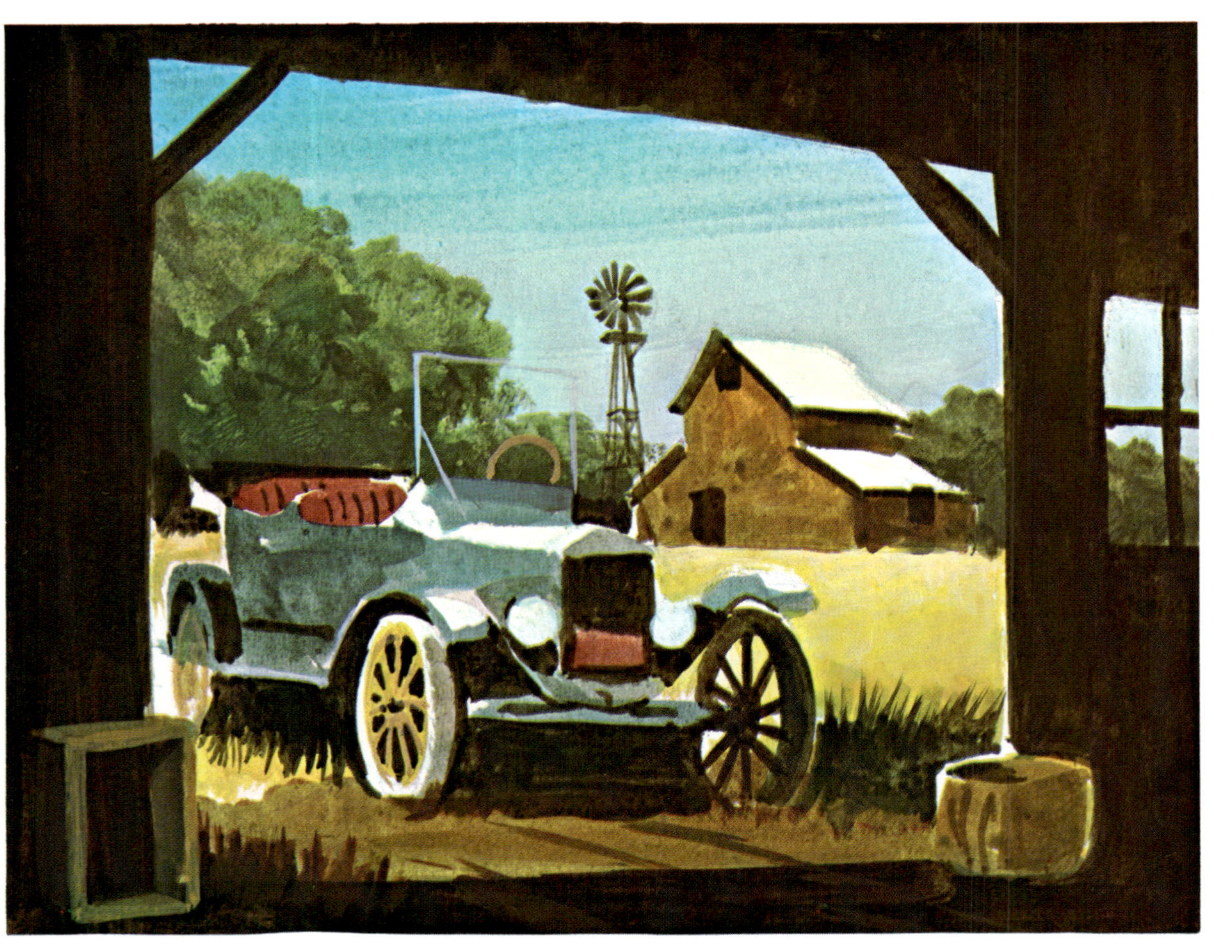

THE OLD MODEL "T"

As you paint, it is very necessary to block in all your colors in rough form. Then you can check the position of your subjects. I really enjoyed using a maximum number of details in this picture. You might even be able to make out the dates on the calendar.

In this painting you are looking out of a dark barn. It gives you a natural border and is interesting.

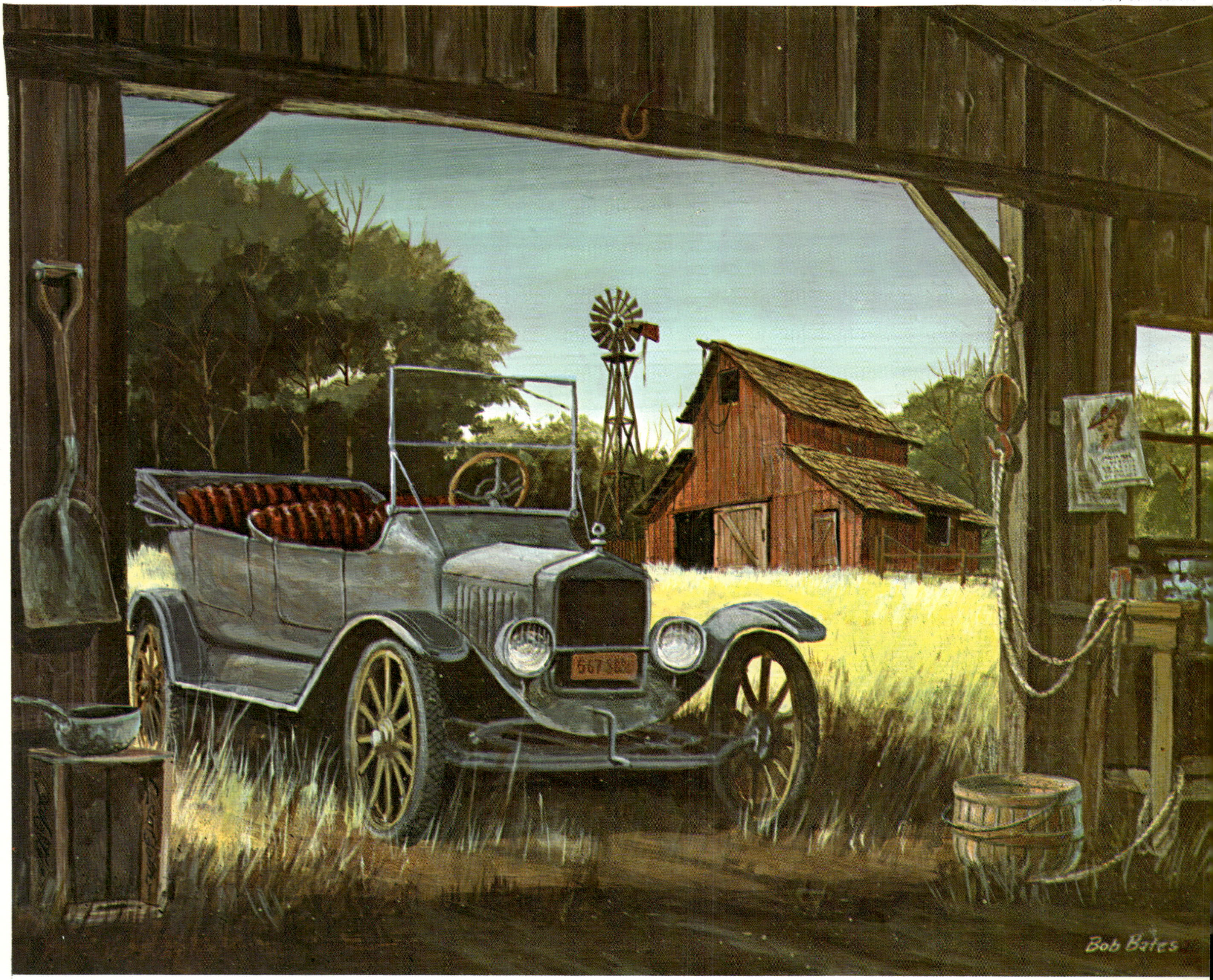

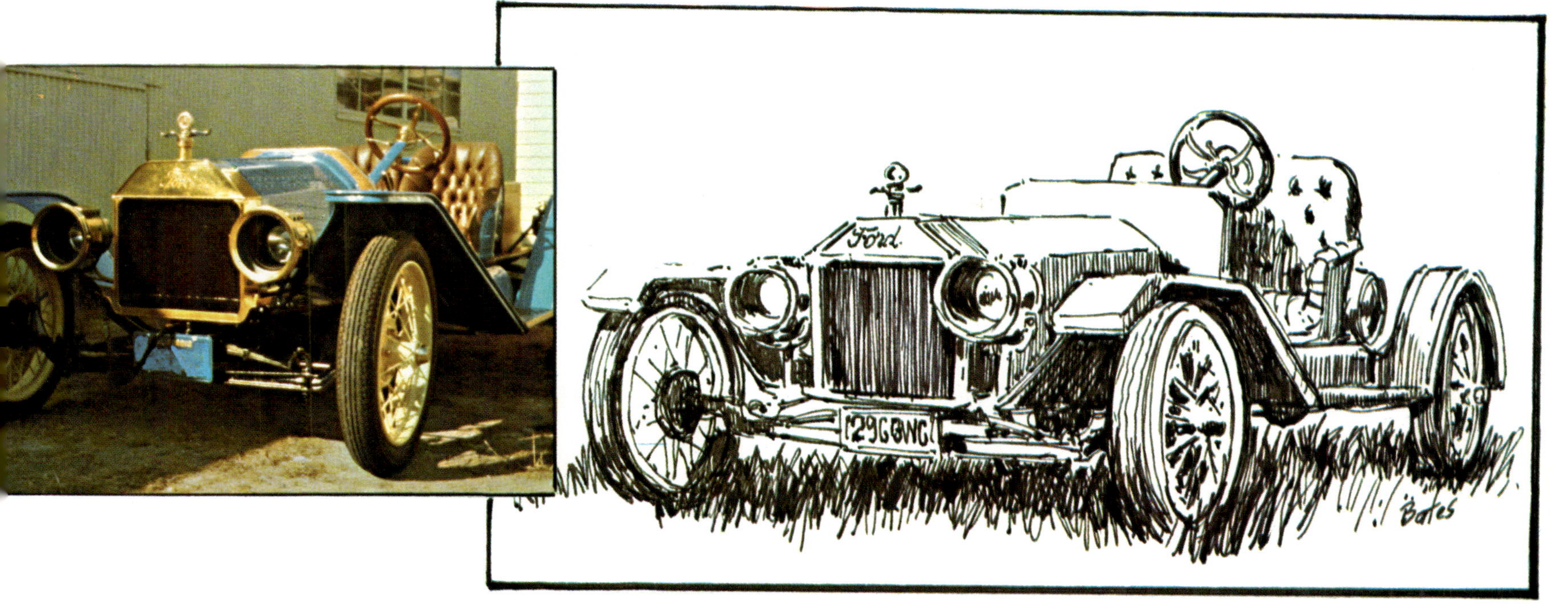

USING THE PHOTO

This beautiful barn is in Henniker, New Hampshire, but the car was found in Newport Beach, Calif. Again we take advantage of photographs and on the spot sketching. The painting was done in the studio.

In this painting you are looking through the barn to the background. This gives you more depth.

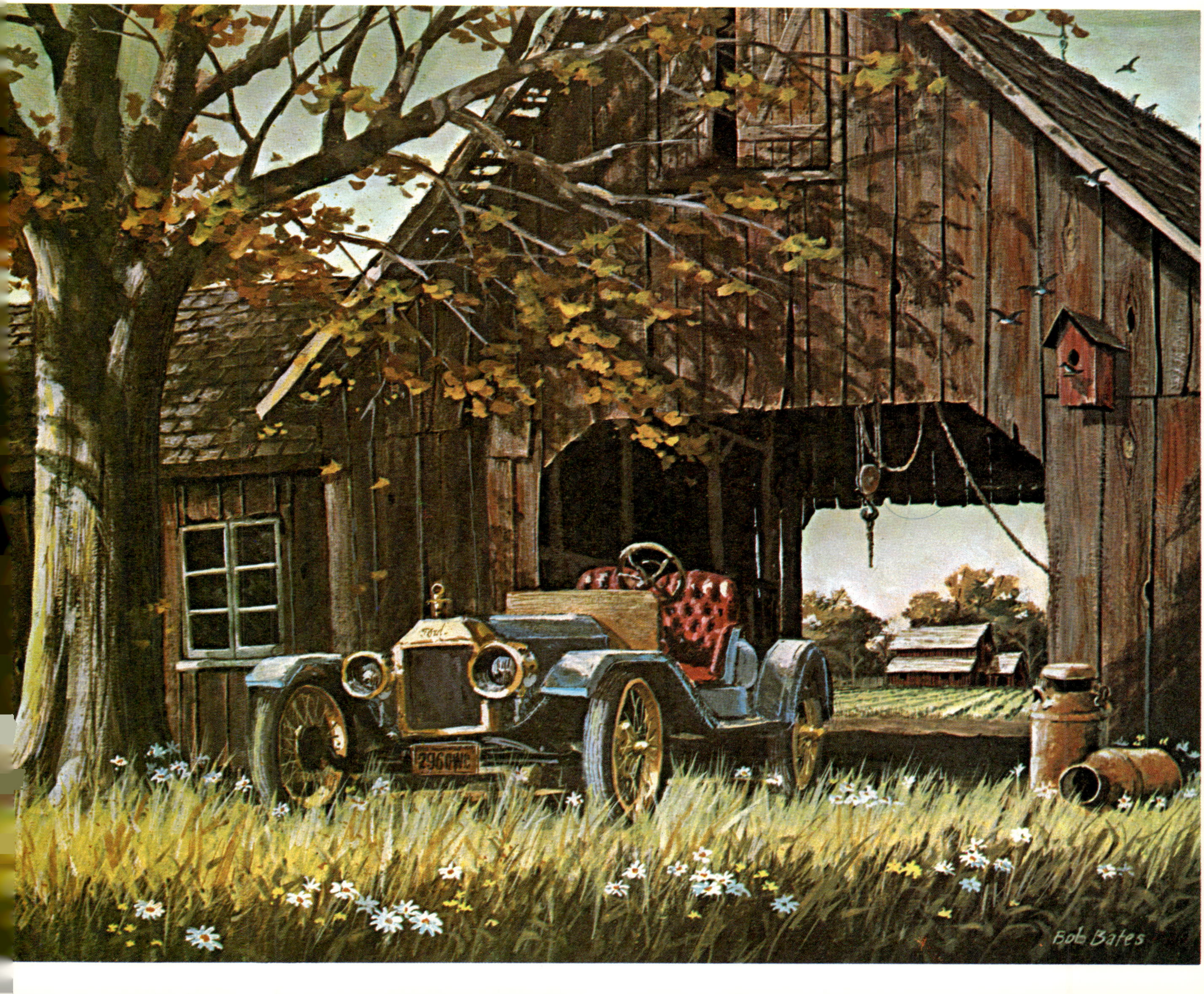

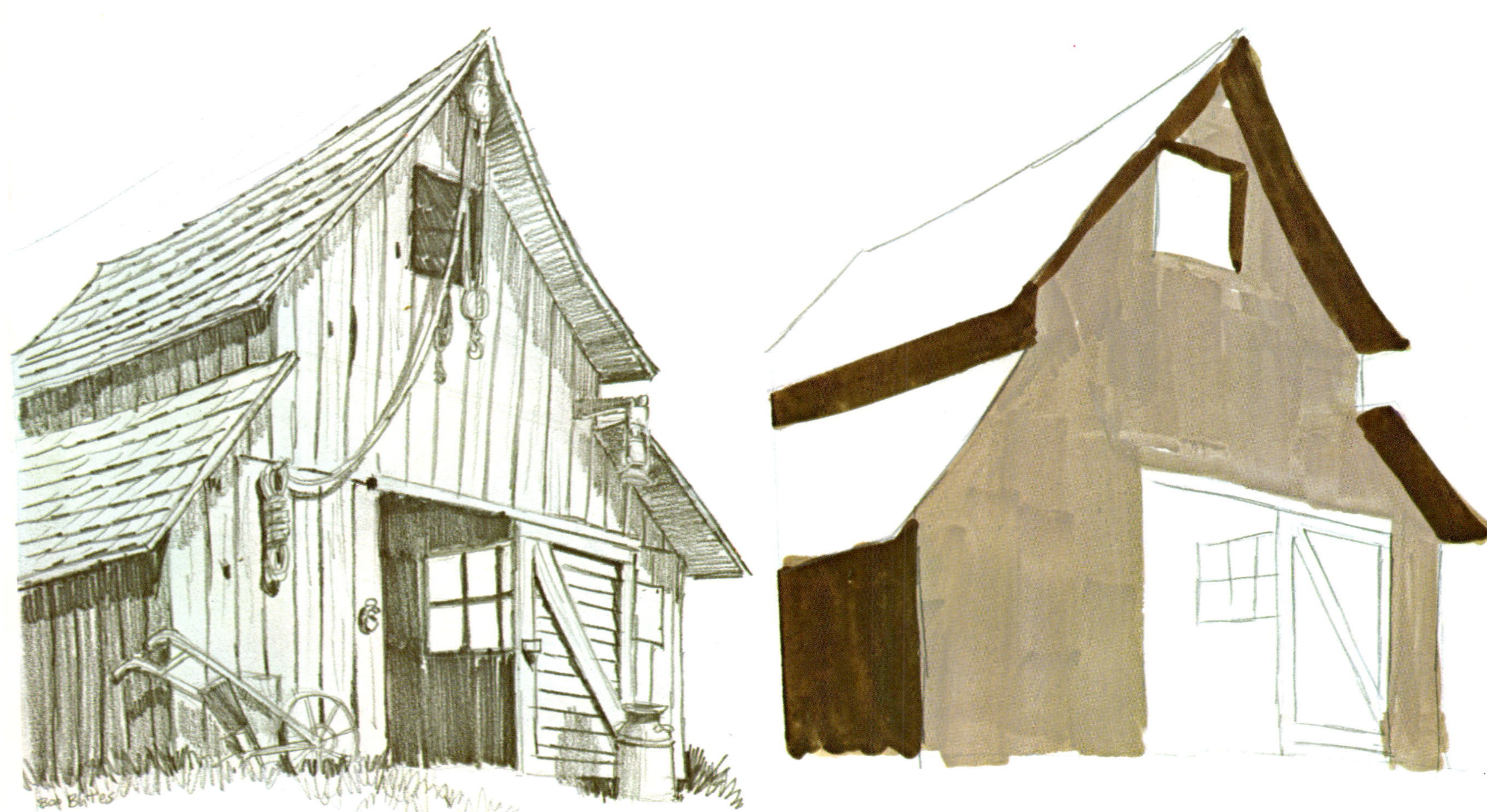

Some items were changed from this pencil sketch to the finished painting.

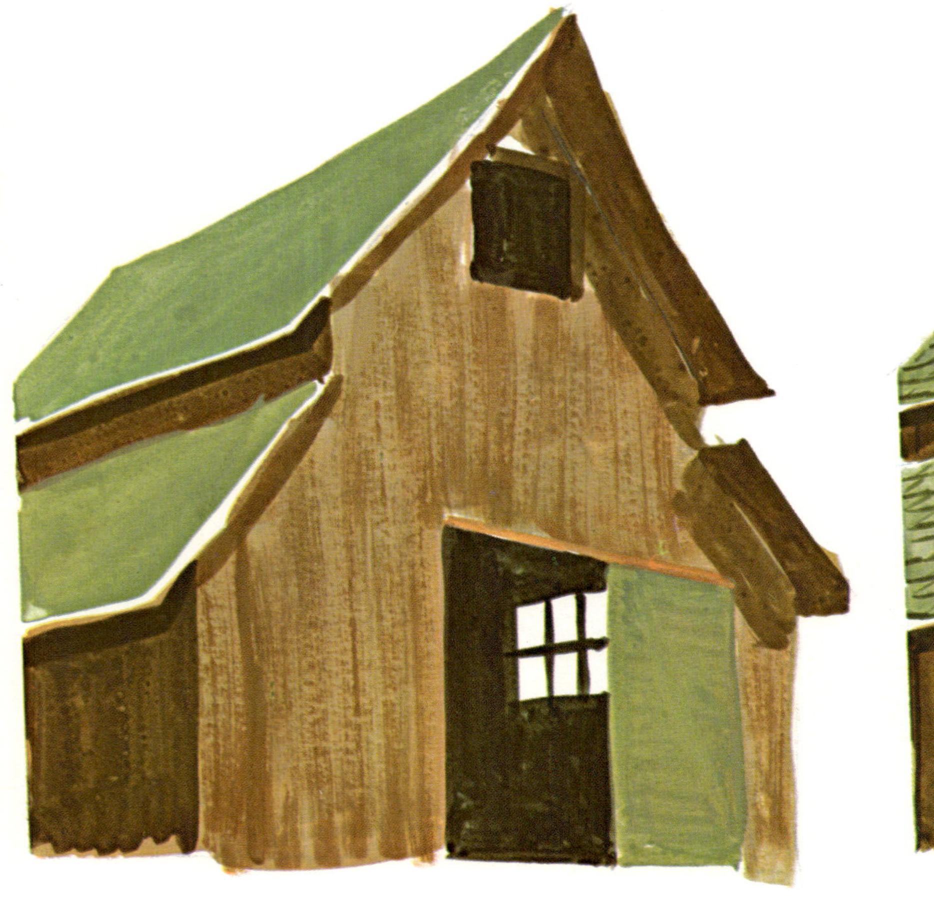

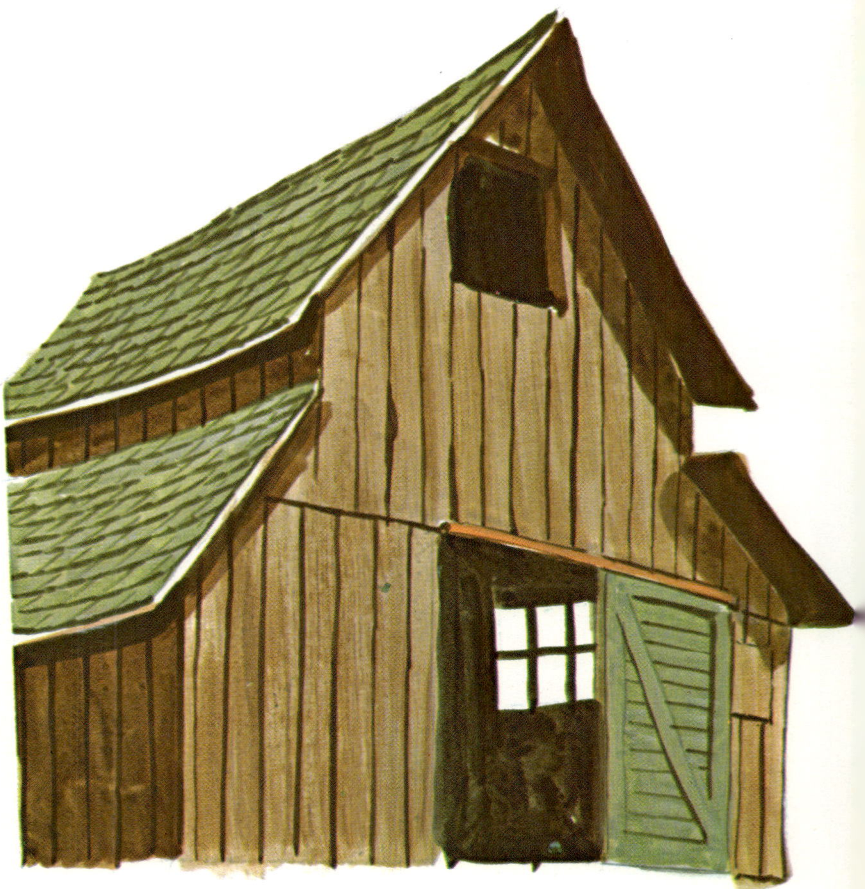

BOB'S BARN

Several years ago I decided to build a barn of my own on my own property. Son Mike, his friend Carl and I tore down an old shed so we were able to have old weathered wood for authenticity. I use the barn in many of my paintings and it also houses my barn antiques.

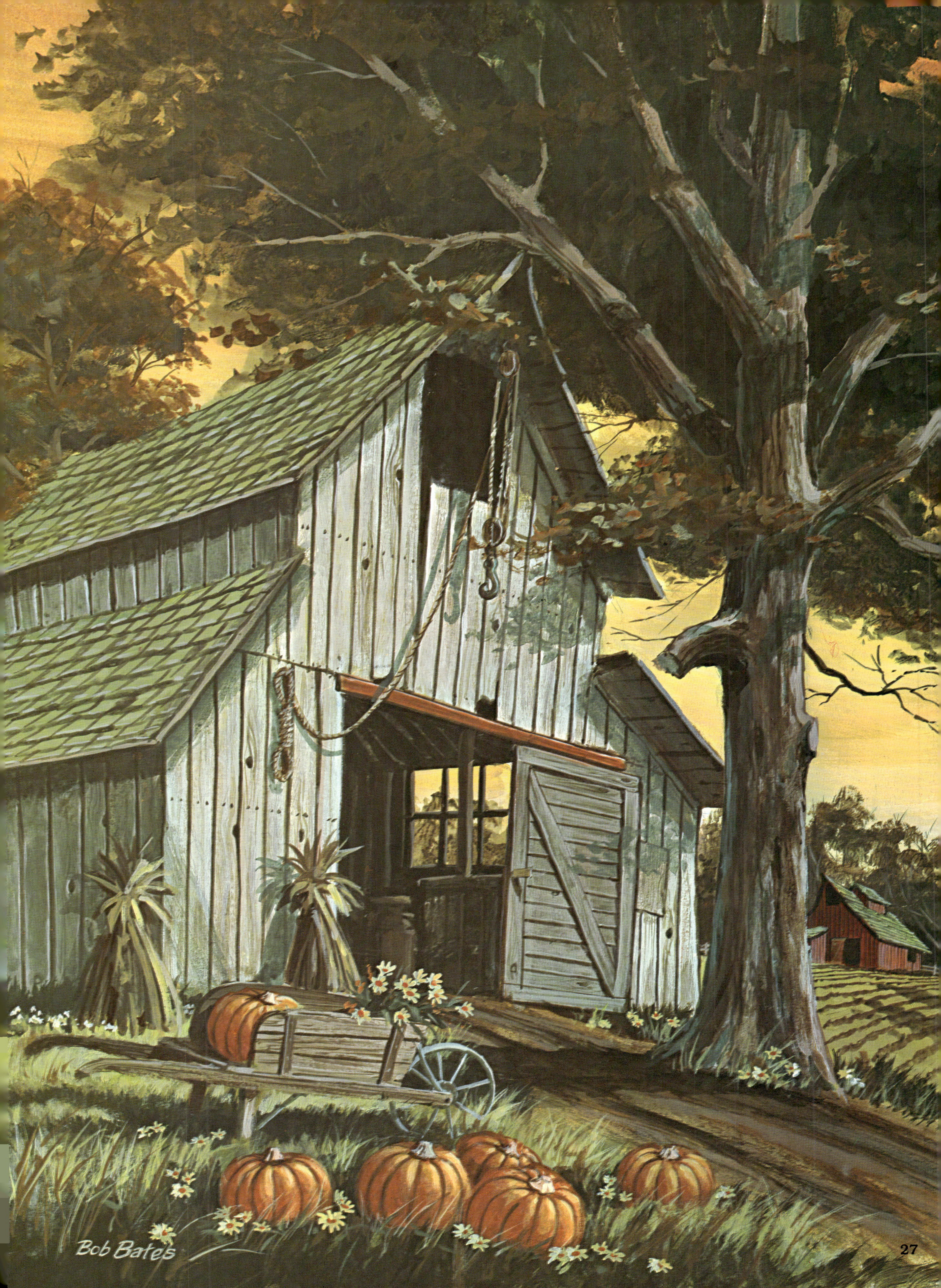
Bob Bates

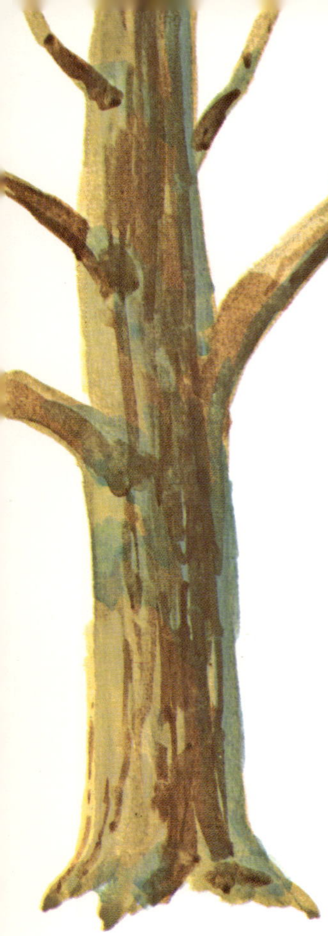

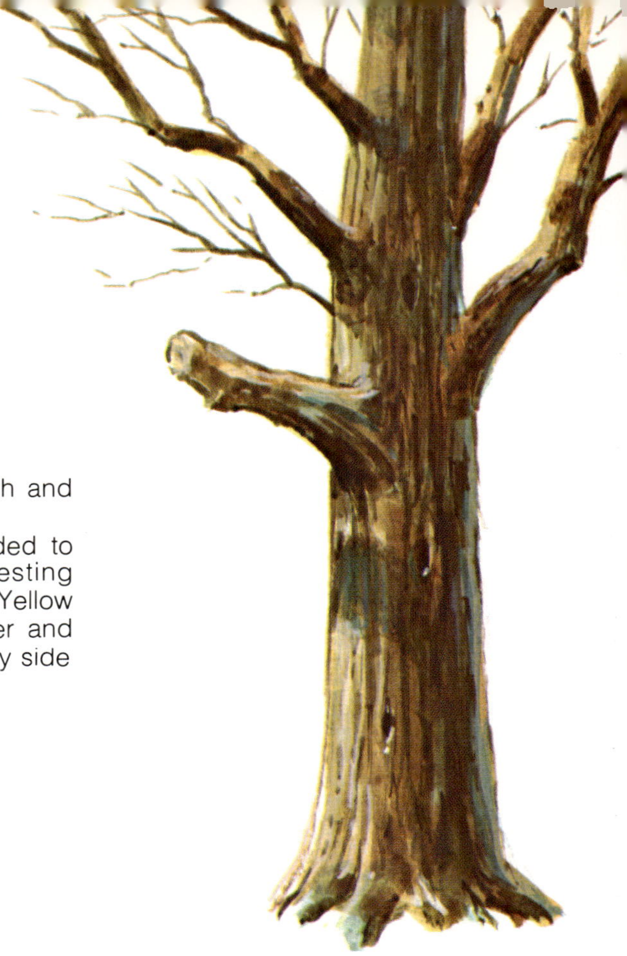

THE TREE TRUNK

A tree in the foreground and to the side can add depth and help border a painting.

Begin with a light grayed-brown with darker color added to the shadow side. The leaves and branches cast interesting shadows. The bark areas on the sunny side have tones of Yellow and Ochre. To give depth to the shadow side, use Umber and thin Black. Now add thin White to the bark on the sunny side and a transparent Blue in the shadows. Good luck!

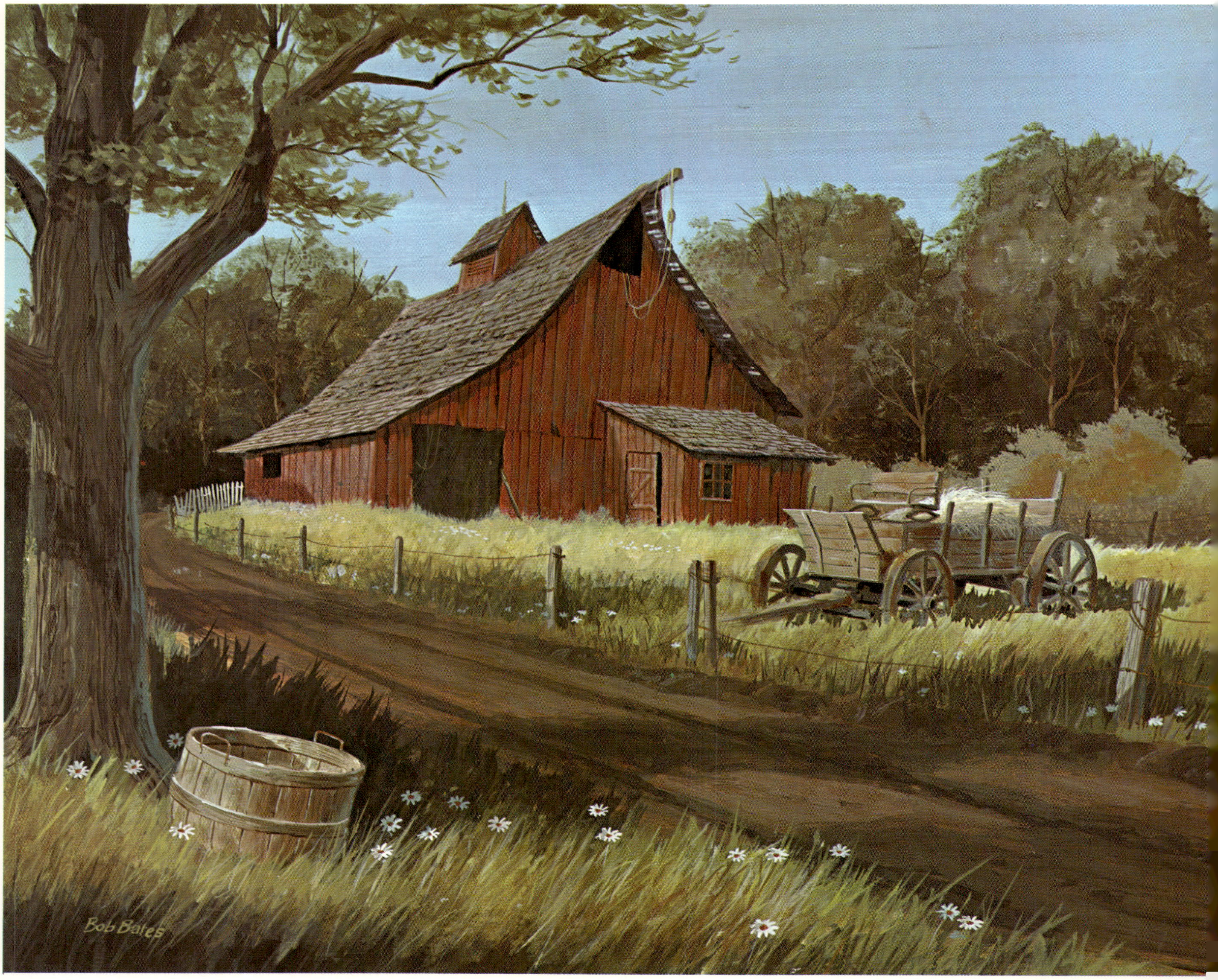

Bob Bates

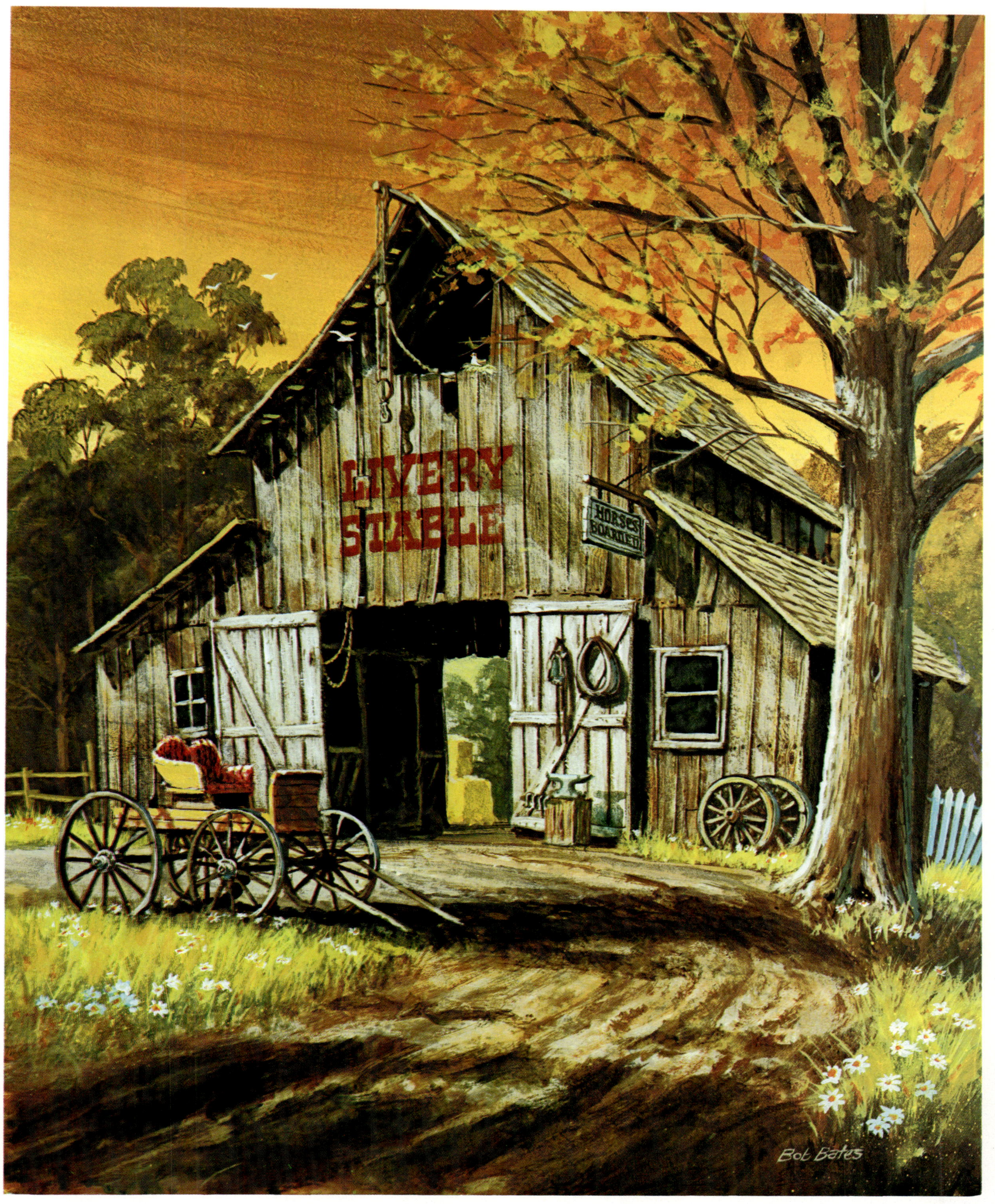

LIVERY STABLE

Nostalgia is the theme in most of my paintings—memories of days gone by—days when the horse was a very important means of transportation.

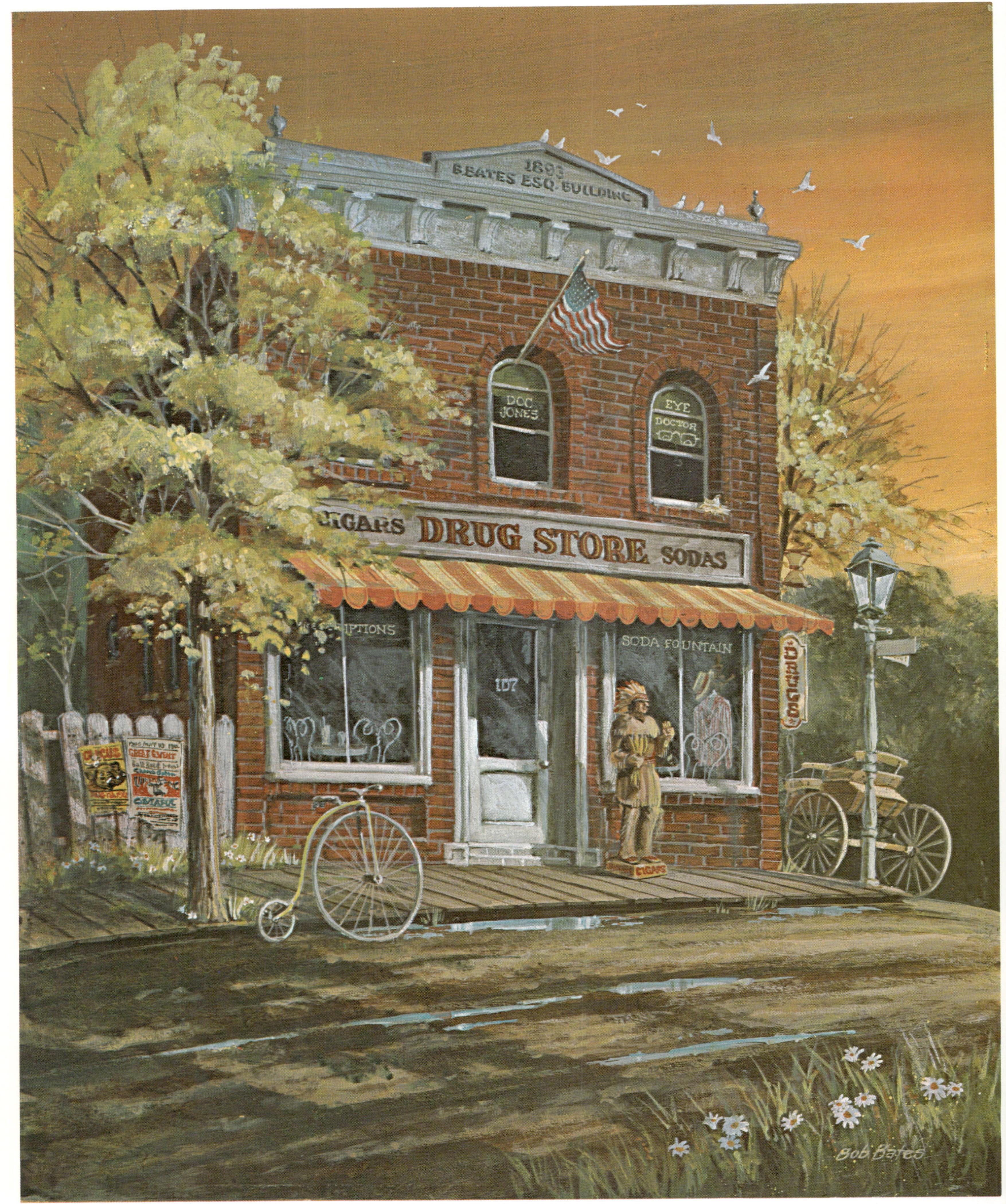

THE CORNER DRUGSTORE

Again we find a picture with an abundance of details added. Except for the basic shape of an old building in Whittier, everything else has either been added or changed.

To paint the interior of this drug store, use Black and Dark Blue and paint the objects in muted tones. For the glass use a glaze of very thin Gray-White. As you paint you can dream yourself back to a quieter time in America.

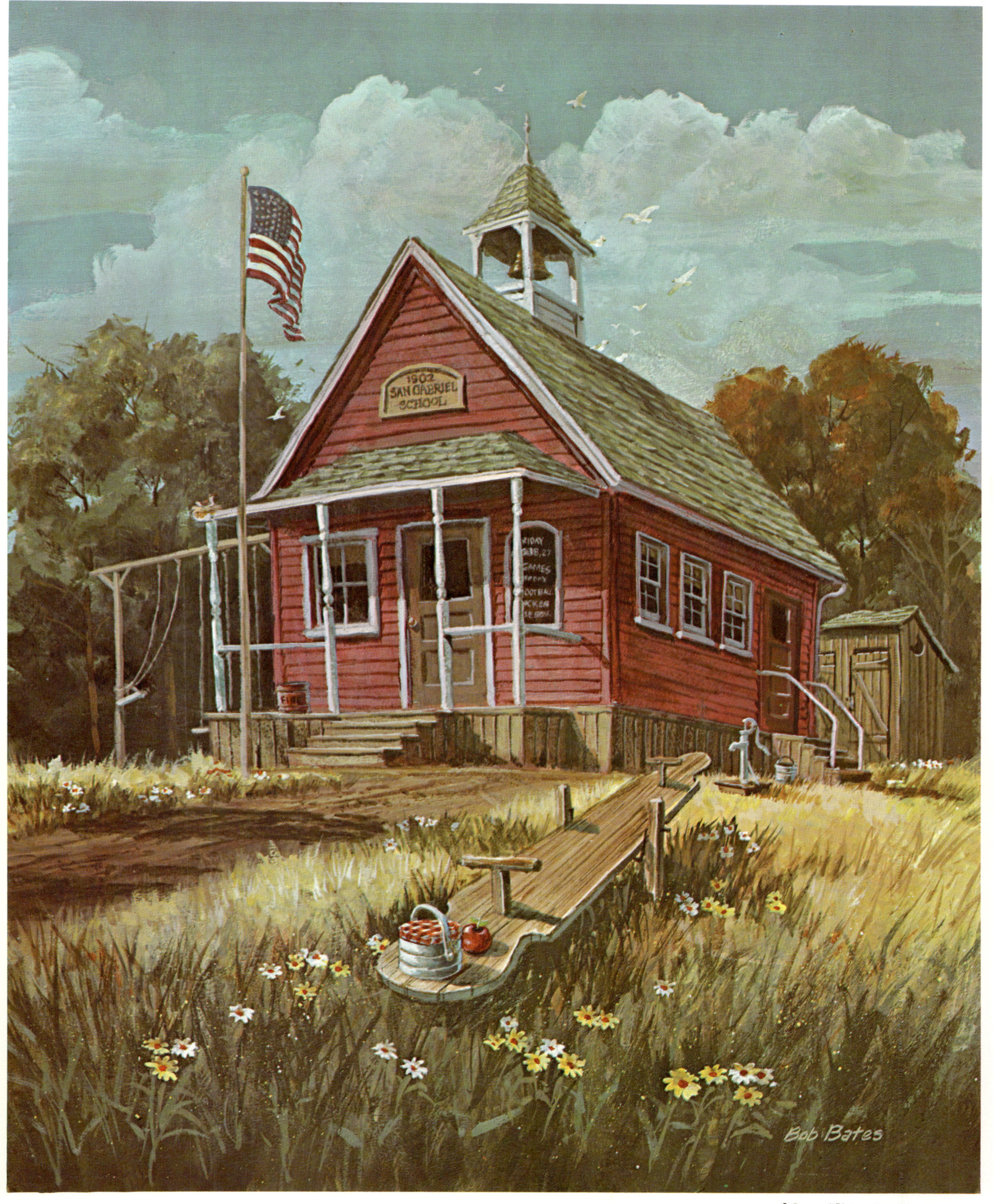

THE OLD SCHOOL HOUSE

Nostalgia again, the one-room school house. This particular one is found in Cambria, California, however, I borrowed the name of my old alma mater. (San Gabriel Ave. School in South Gate, California.)

Painting can be a great pleasure and a marvelous satisfaction. Be bold and adventurous, try not to get discouraged with a few bad paintings, we all have them. Paint subjects you enjoy, and I'm sure your paintings will come out better if you are having fun!

Walter Foster Art Instruction Program

THREE EASY STEPS TO LEARNING ART

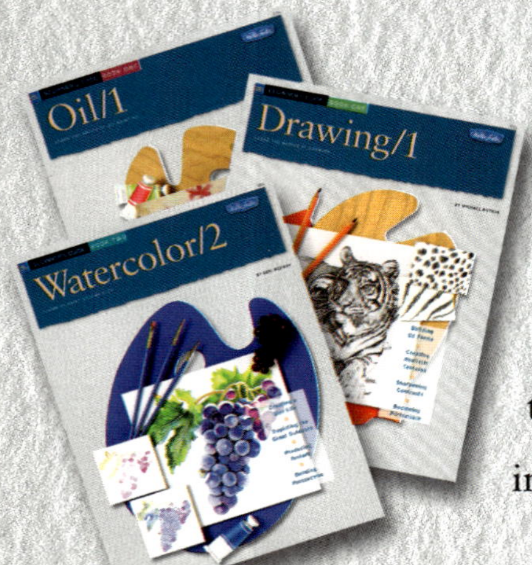

Beginner's Guides are specially written to encourage and motivate aspiring artists. This series introduces the various painting and drawing media—acrylic, oil, pastel, pencil, and watercolor—making it the perfect starting point for beginners. Book One introduces the medium, showing some of its diverse possibilities through beautiful rendered examples and simple explanations, and Book Two instructs with a set of engaging art lessons that follow an easy step-by-step approach.

How to Draw and Paint titles contain progressive visual demonstrations, expert advice, and simple written explanations that assist novice artists through the next stages of learning. In this series, professional artists tap into their experience to walk the reader through the artistic process step by step, from preparation work and preliminary sketches to special techniques and final details. Organized by medium, these books provide insight into an array of subjects.

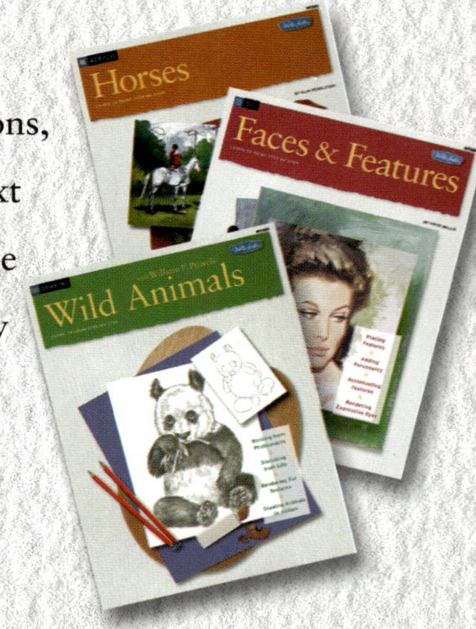

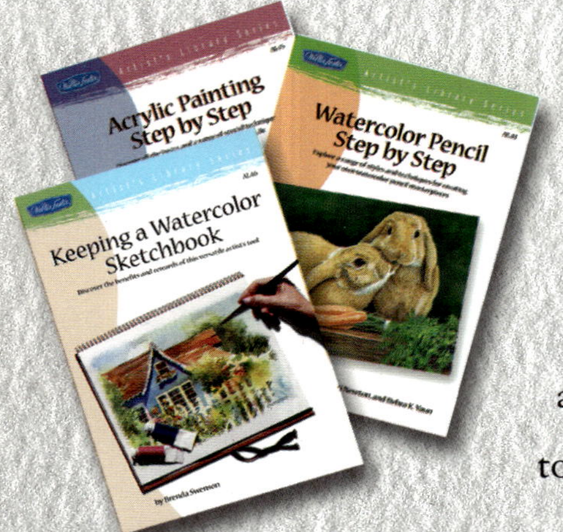

Artist's Library titles offer both beginning and advanced artists the opportunity to expand their creativity, conquer technical obstacles, and explore new media. Written and illustrated by professional artists, the books in this series are ideal for anyone aspiring to reach a new level of expertise. They'll serve as useful tools that artists of all skill levels can refer to again and again.

Walter Foster products are available at art and craft stores everywhere.
For a full list of Walter Foster's titles, visit our website at www.walterfoster.com
or send $5 for a catalog and a $5-off coupon.

WALTER FOSTER PUBLISHING, INC.
23062 La Cadena Drive
Laguna Hills, California 92653
Main Line 949/380-7510
Toll Free 800/426-0099

Walter Foster

www.walterfoster.com